EQ6 BLOCK BOOK

An Illustrated Guide to the Block Patterns in EQ6

The Electric Quilt Company
419 Gould Street, Suite 2
Bowling Green, Ohio 43402

COMPANION BOOK 1

EQ6 Block Book

The Electric Quilt Company
All rights reserved.

The Electric Quilt Company
419 Gould Street, Suite 2
Bowling Green, OH 43402 USA

419/352-1134 (general)
800/356-4219 (sales only)
419/352-4332 (fax)
Find us online at: www.electricquilt.com

Block images from this book were generated by making a grayscale version of the colored block found in the Block Library.

CREDITS:
Book and Cover Design: Sara Seuberling
Book Layout: Heidi Gernheuser

Table of Contents

Classic Pieced 5

Contemporary Pieced 57

Foundation Pieced 89

Classic Appliqué 129

Contemporary Appliqué 147

Motifs 177

Quilting Stencils 199

Overlaid Blocks 213

Border Blocks 221

Reference Information and Index 243

Electric Quilt 6

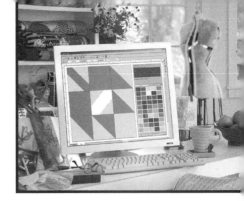

1 Classic Pieced

Album (Autograph) Blocks 6

Alphabet (Modified) 7

Alphabet (Traditional) 8

Antique Mosaics 10

Baskets (Traditional) 11

Chains 12

Classics 14

Compasses 15

Diamond in Square 16

Dresden Fan (Blades) 18

Dresden Fan (Petals) 19

Dresden Four Fans 20

Dresden Plate (Blades) 22

Dresden Plate (Petals) 23

Drunkard's Path 24

Eccentrics 25

Eight-Pointed Stars 26

Feathered Stars 28

Five- and Six-Pointed Stars 29

Five Patch 30

Four Patch 32

Four X 34

Ladies Art Company 35

Lone Stars 37

Maltese Cross 39

Nine Patch 40

Nine Patch Stars 42

Old Favorites 44

Orange Peels 45

Pickles and Rings 46

Pictures 47

Priscilla 49

Simple Blocks 50

Stars 52

Variable Stars 53

Wheels 54

Whole Top Designs 55

Leaf Album Block

New Album Variation

Album Block

Album-Variable Star

Album-Variable Star II

Album-Variable Star III

Album-Variable Star IV

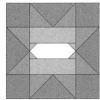

Album-Variable Star V

Album-Variable Star VI

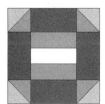

Album-Churn Dash Variation

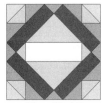

Album Block II

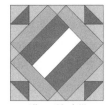

Album Block III

Album Block IV

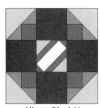

Album Block V

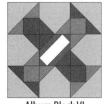

Album Block VI

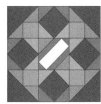

Album Block VII

Album Block VIII

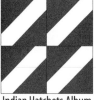

Indian Hatchets Album Block

Nine Patch Album Block

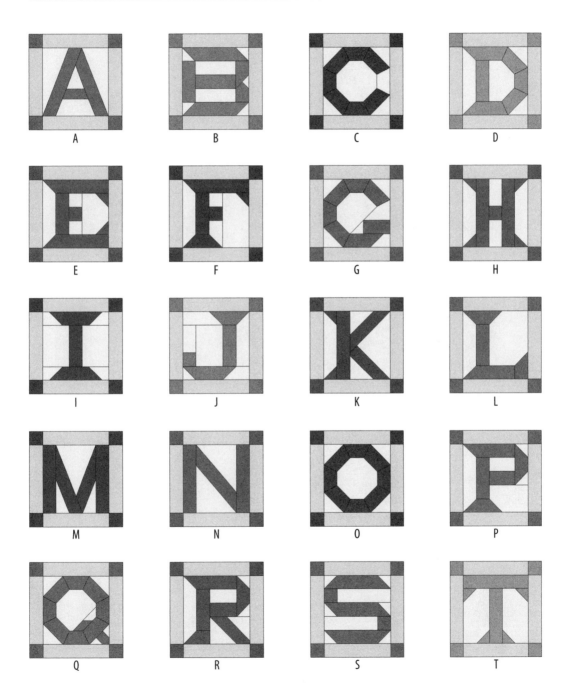

A

B

C

D

E

F

G

H

I

J

K

L

M

N

O

P

Q

R

S

T

U	V	W	X
Y	Z	One	Two
Three	Four	Five	Six
Seven	Eight	Nine	Zero

1 Classic Pieced

Alphabet (Traditional)

 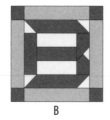 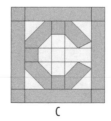 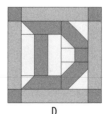

A	B	C	D

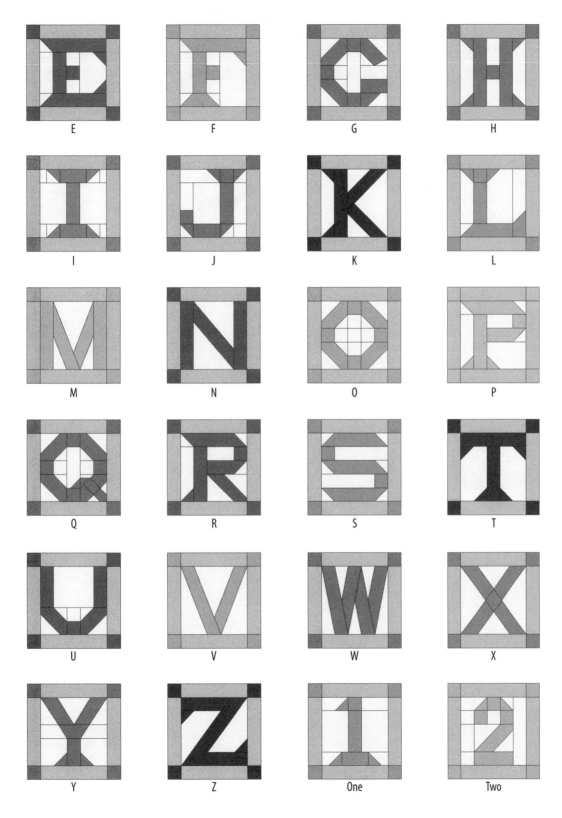

E	F	G	H
I	J	K	L
M	N	O	P
Q	R	S	T
U	V	W	X
Y	Z	One	Two

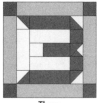

Three

Four

Five

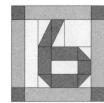

Six

Seven

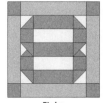

Eight

Nine

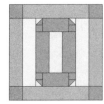

Zero

1 Classic Pieced
Antique Mosaics

Mosaic, No. 1

Mosaic, No. 1 (2)

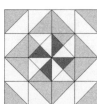

Mosaic, No. 2

Mosaic, No. 2 (2)

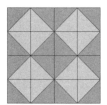

Mosaic, No. 3

Mosaic, No. 3 (2)

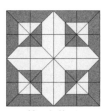

Mosaic, No. 4

Mosaic, No. 4 (2)

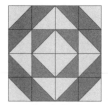

Mosaic, No. 5

Mosaic, No. 5 (2)

Mosaic, No. 6 (6)

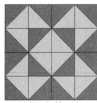

Mosaic, No. 10

Mosaic, No. 10 (2)

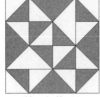
Mosaic, No. 11

Mosaic, No. 13

Mosaic, No. 13 (2)

Mosaic, No. 15

Mosaic, No. 17

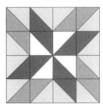
Mosaic, No. 18

Mosaic, No. 18 (2)

Mosaic, No. 19

Mosaic, No. 19 (2)

Mosaic, No. 19 Variation

Mosaic, No. 20

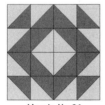
Mosaic, No. 21

Mosaic, No. 21 (2)

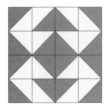
Mosaic, No. 22

1 Classic Pieced
Baskets (Traditional)

Tulip Basket

Tulip Basket Variation

Potted Star Flower

Potted Star Flower
Variation

Basket of Lilies

Tulip Basket

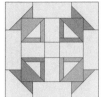

Four Little Baskets

Fruit Basket

Basket of Flowers

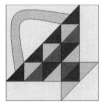

Four Little Baskets

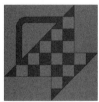

Garden Basket
Variation

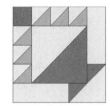

Flower Basket

Basket

Basket with Handles

Basket with Handles

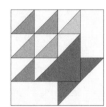

Basket

1 Classic Pieced
Chains

Four Patch

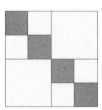

Double Four Patch

Hour Glass

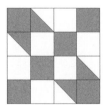

Road to Oklahoma

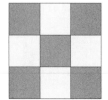

Nine Patch

Double Nine Patch

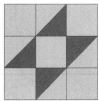

Road to California

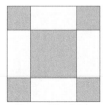

Uneven Nine Patch

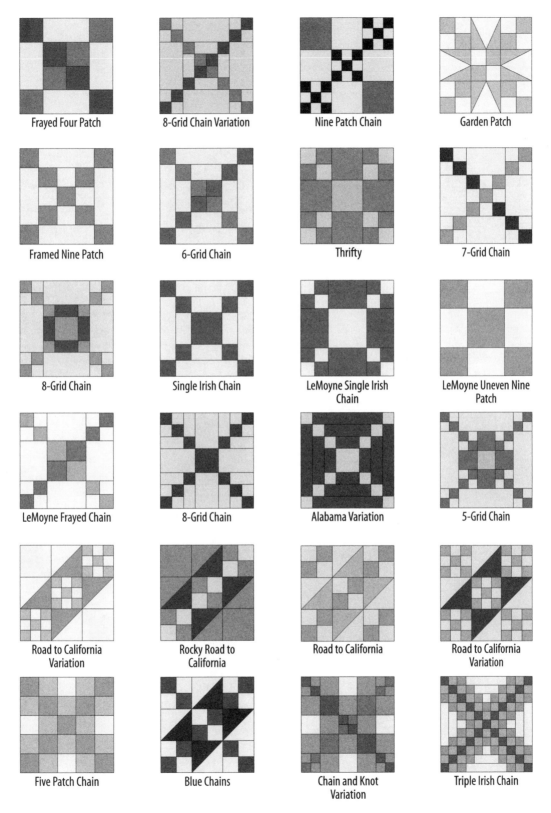

Frayed Four Patch

8-Grid Chain Variation

Nine Patch Chain

Garden Patch

Framed Nine Patch

6-Grid Chain

Thrifty

7-Grid Chain

8-Grid Chain

Single Irish Chain

LeMoyne Single Irish Chain

LeMoyne Uneven Nine Patch

LeMoyne Frayed Chain

8-Grid Chain

Alabama Variation

5-Grid Chain

Road to California Variation

Rocky Road to California

Road to California

Road to California Variation

Five Patch Chain

Blue Chains

Chain and Knot Variation

Triple Irish Chain

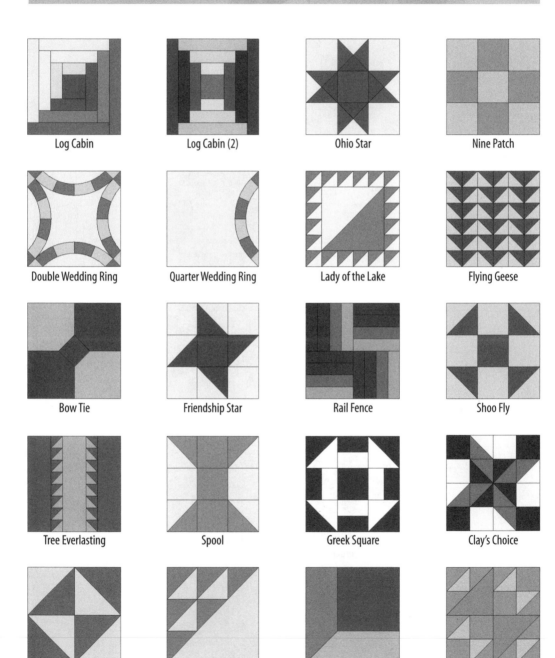

Log Cabin

Log Cabin (2)

Ohio Star

Nine Patch

Double Wedding Ring

Quarter Wedding Ring

Lady of the Lake

Flying Geese

Bow Tie

Friendship Star

Rail Fence

Shoo Fly

Tree Everlasting

Spool

Greek Square

Clay's Choice

Broken Dishes

Birds in the Air

Attic Window

Old Maid's Puzzle

Whirlwind

Pin Wheels

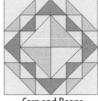

Corn and Beans

Road to Oklahoma

Cross and Crown

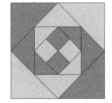

Bear's Paw

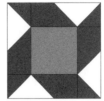

Churn Dash

Indian Hatchets

Wild Goose Chase

Monkey Wrench

1 Classic Pieced

Compasses

Mariner's Star

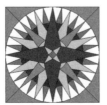

Compass Star

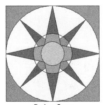

Daisy Star

Sunburst

Chips and Whetstones

Mariner's Compass

Mariner's Compass

Star Wheel

Circle Star

Southern Star

Rising Sun

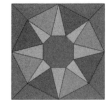

Rising Star

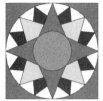

Circle Star

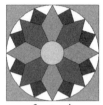

Courtyard

Compass Points

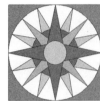

Sunrise

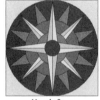

North Star

Georgetown Circle

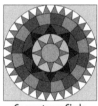

Georgetown Circle Variation

Georgetown Circle Variation

Mariner's Compass

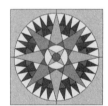

Mariner's Compass

1 Classic Pieced

Diamond in Square

Diamond in the Square

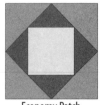

Economy Patch

Twelve Triangles

Square in a Square

Mosaic

Double Cross

Triple Stripe

Mother's Dream

Susannah (Variation)

Susannah (Variation)

Susannah (Variation)

Improved Four Patch

Coffin Star

Grandmother's Cross

Coxey's Camp

New Album

Art Square

Right and Left

Sugar Bowl

Cross with a Cross

King's Crown

Monkey Wrench

Snail's Trail

Contrary Wife

Contrary Wife Variation

Improved Nine Patch

Four Patch Art Square

Nine Patch Art Square

Four Times Four

Four Times Nine

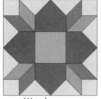

Weathervane

Weathervane Variation

Arbor Window

1 Classic Pieced

Dresden Fan (Blades)

3 Blade Dresden Flower Fan

4 Blade Dresden Flower Fan

5 Blade Dresden Flower Fan

6 Blade Dresden Flower Fan

7 Blade Dresden Flower Fan

8 Blade Dresden Flower Fan

3 Blade Dresden Fan

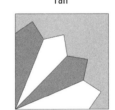

4 Blade Dresden Fan

5 Blade Dresden Fan

6 Blade Dresden Fan

7 Blade Dresden Fan

8 Blade Dresden Fan

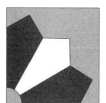

3 Blade Small Center
Dresden Fan

4 Blade Small Center
Dresden Fan

5 Blade Small Center
Dresden Fan

6 Blade Small Center
Dresden Fan

7 Blade Small Center
Dresden Fan

8 Blade Small Center
Dresden Fan

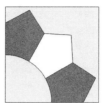

3 Blade Large Center
Dresden Fan

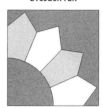

4 Blade Large Center
Dresden Fan

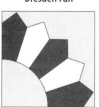

5 Blade Large Center
Dresden Fan

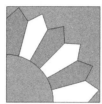

6 Blade Large Center
Dresden Fan

7 Blade Large Center
Dresden Fan

8 Blade Large Center
Dresden Fan

1 Classic Pieced

Dresden Fan (Petals)

3 Petal Dresden Flower
Fan

4 Petal Dresden Flower
Fan

5 Petal Dresden Flower
Fan

6 Petal Dresden Flower
Fan

7 Petal Dresden Flower
Fan

8 Petal Dresden Flower
Fan

3 Petal Dresden Fan

4 Petal Dresden Fan

5 Petal Dresden Fan

6 Petal Dresden Fan

7 Petal Dresden Fan

8 Petal Dresden Fan

3 Petal Small Center
Dresden Fan

4 Petal Small Center
Dresden Fan

5 Petal Small Center
Dresden Fan

6 Petal Small Center
Dresden Fan

7 Petal Small Center
Dresden Fan

8 Petal Small Center
Dresden Fan

3 Petal Large Center
Dresden Fan

4 Petal Large Center
Dresden Fan

5 Petal Large Center
Dresden Fan

6 Petal Large Center
Dresden Fan

7 Petal Large Center
Dresden Fan

8 Petal Large Center
Dresden Fan

1 Classic Pieced

Dresden Four Fans

Four Fans Six Petals

Four Fans Four Blades

Four Fans Three Petals

Four Fans Nine Blades

Four Fans Seven Petals

Four Fans Three Blades

Four Fans Five Petals

Four Fans Seven Blades

Four Fans Four Petals

Four Fans Six Blades

Four Fans Four Petals

Four Fans Eight Blades

Four Fans Four Blades

Four Fans Six Petals

Four Fans Five Blades

Four Fans Six Blades

Four Fans Eight Petals

Four Fans Nine Petals

Four Fans Five Blades

Four Fans Five Petals

Four Fans Eight Blades

Four Fans Eight Petals

Four Fans Eight Blades

Four Fans Eight Petals

Four Fans Three Petals

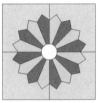

Classic Dresden Bladed Plate

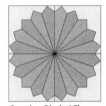

Dresden Bladed Flower

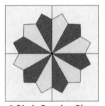

3 Blade Dresden Plate

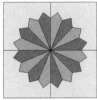

4 Blade Dresden Plate

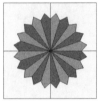

5 Blade Dresden Plate

6 Blade Dresden Plate

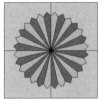

7 Blade Dresden Plate

8 Blade Dresden Plate

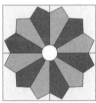

3 Blade Small Center Dresden Plate

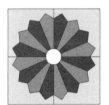

4 Blade Small Center Dresden Plate

5 Blade Small Center Dresden Plate

6 Blade Small Center Dresden Plate

7 Blade Small Center Dresden Plate

8 Blade Small Center Dresden Plate

3 Blade Large Center Dresden Plate

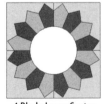

4 Blade Large Center Dresden Plate

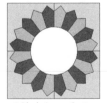

5 Blade Large Center Dresden Plate

6 Blade Large Center Dresden Plate

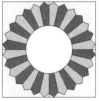

7 Blade Large Center Dresden Plate

8 Blade Large Center Dresden Plate

Dresden Plate (Petals)

Classic Dresden Plate

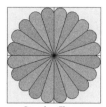
Dresden Flower

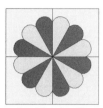
3 Petal Dresden Plate

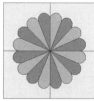
4 Petal Dresden Plate

5 Petal Dresden Plate

6 Petal Dresden Plate

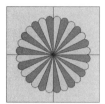
7 Petal Dresden Plate

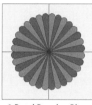
8 Petal Dresden Plate

3 Petal Small Center
Dresden Plate

4 Petal Small Center
Dresden Plate

5 Petal Small Center
Dresden Plate

6 Petal Small Center
Dresden Plate

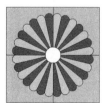
7 Petal Small Center
Dresden Plate

8 Petal Small Center
Dresden Plate

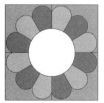
3 Petal Large Center
Dresden Plate

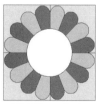
4 Petal Large Center
Dresden Plate

5 Petal Large Center
Dresden Plate

6 Petal Large Center
Dresden Plate

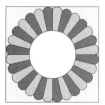
7 Petal Large Center
Dresden Plate

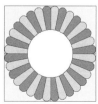
8 Petal Large Center
Dresden Plate

Drunkard's Path

Drunkard's Path

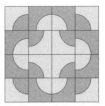

Cleopatra's Puzzle

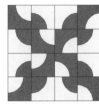

Drunkard's Path

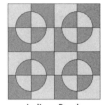

Indiana Puzzle

Falling Timbers

Around the World

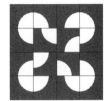

Fool's Puzzle

Dove

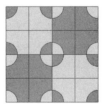

Millwheel

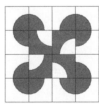

I Wish You Well

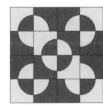

Drunkard's Path Variation

Steeplechase

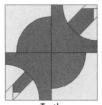

Turtle

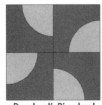

Drunkard's Pinwheel

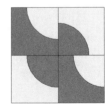

Peace Dove

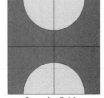

Over the Bridge

Around the World

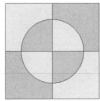

Baseball

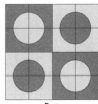

Dots

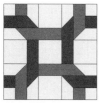

Plaited Block Variation

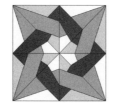

Tangled Stars

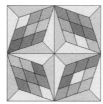

Four Block Star

Paducah Peony

Ribbons

Washington's Puzzle

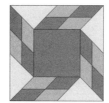

Slashed Album

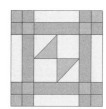

Odds and Ends

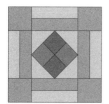

Coxey's Camp

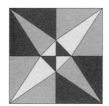

Crossed Canoes

Ribbon Border

Right and Left

Work Box

Tangled Lines

Double Pinwheel
Whirls

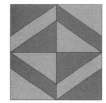

Left and Right

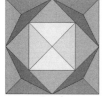

Jewel

The Priscilla
(PatchDraw)

The Priscilla (EasyDraw)

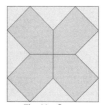

The Mayflower

LeMoyne Star

Eight Point Star
(PatchDraw)

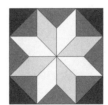

LeMoyne Star 2

LeMoyne Star 3

LeMoyne Star 4

Star of the East

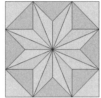

Silver and Gold

St. Louis Star Variation

Rolling Star

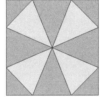

Kaleidoscope

Kaleidoscope 2

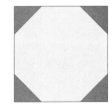

Octagon

Star Variation

Blazing Star

Wrapped Star
(PatchDraw)

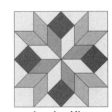

Love in a Mist

Royal Diamonds

Pole Star

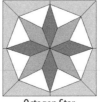

Octagon Star

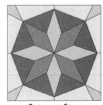

Octagon Star

Western Spy

Ohio Star Variation

LeMoyne Star Variation

Andrea's LeMoyne

Spiderweb Star 2

Four Stars Patchwork

Four Stars Patchwork
Variation

Starlight

Starlight Variation

Star of Bethlehem

Rolling Star

Dutch Rose

Carpenter's Wheel

Rolling Star

Lena's Choice

Spiderweb Star

Birds and Star

Boxed Star

Stars and Lilies

Star Flowers

Shooting Star

Rick-Rack Star

Starry Night

Four Stars Bordered

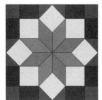

Cornered Star

1 Classic Pieced

Feathered Stars

Radiant Star

Peaceful Hours

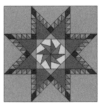

Pinwheel Star

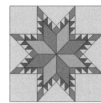

Feathered LeMoyne

Square-in-Square Star

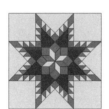

Feathered Star in Star

Snowflake Feathered Star

Rolling Feathered Star

Feathered Sunflower Star

Feathered Star

Star of Bethlehem

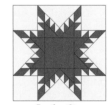

Feather Star

Ohio Feathered Star

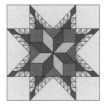

Feathered Star

Shooting Stars

California Friendship Star

Union Star

Five-Point Star

Five-Point Star

Five Pointed Star

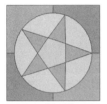

Star of the West

Star and Crescent

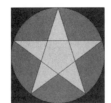

Five-Pointed Star

Five-Pointed Star

Pentagon Star

Savannah Beautiful
Star

Nine by Six

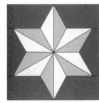

Star of the East

Star of Bethlehem

Origami Star

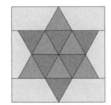

Six-Pointed Star

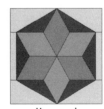

Hexagonal

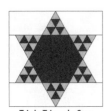

Triple Triangle Star

Columbia

Pentagon Star 2

Circled Star

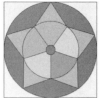

Divided Star

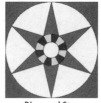

Diamond Star

Star-in-Star

Stars and Arcs

1 Classic Pieced
Five Patch

Twenty-Five Patch

Five Patch Shoo Fly

Cross and Crown

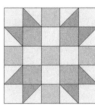

Four X Star

Goose Tracks

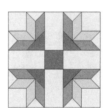

Goose Tracks Variation

Lady of the Lake

Flying Squares

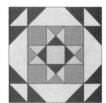

Square and a Half

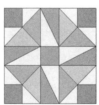

Pinwheel Square

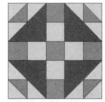

Duck and Ducklings

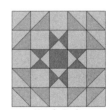

Handy Andy

Bird's Nest

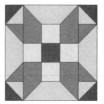

Fool's Square

St. Louis Star

Children's Delight

King's Crown

Red Cross

Crazy House

Clown

Providence Quilt Block

Goose in the Pond

Grandmother's Puzzle

Sister's Choice

Album Quilt

Premium Star

Fanny's Fan

Odd Scraps Patchwork

Game Cocks

Missouri Puzzle

King's Chain

Five Patch Chain

Grandma's Favorite

Garden of Eden

Nine Patch Star

Nine Patch Star
Variation

1 Classic Pieced
Four Patch

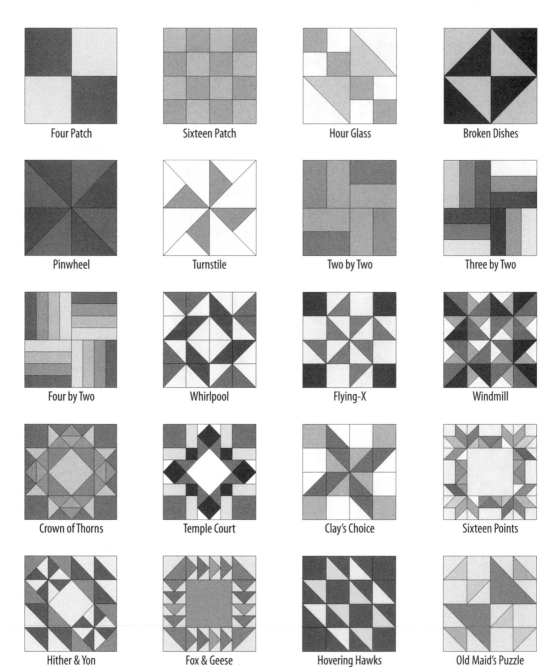

Four Patch	Sixteen Patch	Hour Glass	Broken Dishes
Pinwheel	Turnstile	Two by Two	Three by Two
Four by Two	Whirlpool	Flying-X	Windmill
Crown of Thorns	Temple Court	Clay's Choice	Sixteen Points
Hither & Yon	Fox & Geese	Hovering Hawks	Old Maid's Puzzle

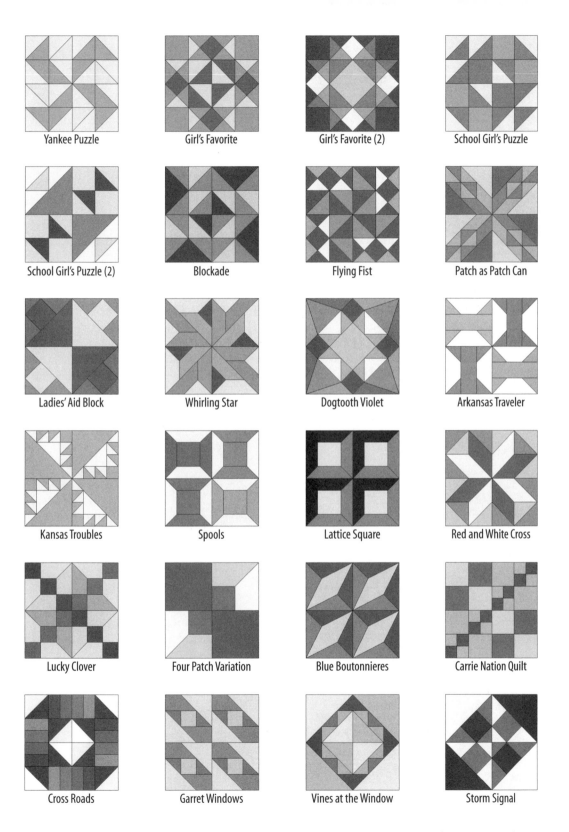

Yankee Puzzle

Girl's Favorite

Girl's Favorite (2)

School Girl's Puzzle

School Girl's Puzzle (2)

Blockade

Flying Fist

Patch as Patch Can

Ladies' Aid Block

Whirling Star

Dogtooth Violet

Arkansas Traveler

Kansas Troubles

Spools

Lattice Square

Red and White Cross

Lucky Clover

Four Patch Variation

Blue Boutonnieres

Carrie Nation Quilt

Cross Roads

Garret Windows

Vines at the Window

Storm Signal

Dad's Bow Tie

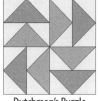

Dutchman's Puzzle

White Cross

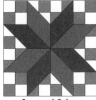

Star and Cubes

True Lover's Knot

1 Classic Pieced
Four X

Basic 4X

Y Block

Checkerboard

Half Checkerboard

Boise

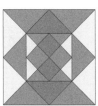

Cock's Comb

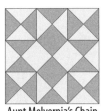

Aunt Melvernia's Chain

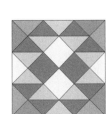

Buckwheat

Four X Variation

Granny's Choice (Adap.)

The Arrowhead

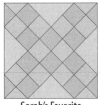

Sarah's Favorite

New Hour Glass

Twin Sisters

Twin Sisters Variation

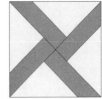

Windmill and Outline

Criss Cross Variation

Criss Cross Variation

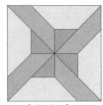

Spinning Stars
Variation

Good Luck

Mill and Stars

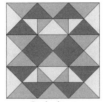

Buckwheat

1 Classic Pieced

Ladies Art Company

Merry Kite

Star of North Carolina

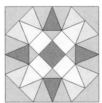

Star of North Carolina
Variation

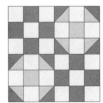

Flagstones

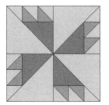

Rosebud

Hand Weave

All Kinds

Linton

Roman Cross

Propeller

Lost Ship Pattern

Texas Flower

Cross within Cross

Widower's Choice

Bird's Nest

Navajo

Baton Rouge Block

Santa Fe Block

Magic Circle

Album

Double Z

Storm at Sea

Chicago Star

Devil's Puzzle

Star and Chains

World's Fair Puzzle

New Star

Wheel of Fortune

Crosses and Star

Bat's Wings

Cut Glass Dish

Double X, No.1

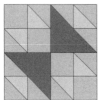

Double X, No.2

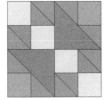

Double X, No.3

Double X, No.4

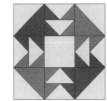

Capital T

Texas Tears

Old Maid's Ramble

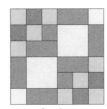

Domino

Letter H

W.C.T. Union

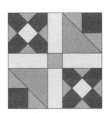

Leap Frog

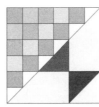

Steps to the Altar

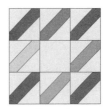

Nonsuch

A Snowflake

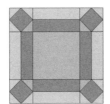

Johnnie-Round-the-Corner

T Quartette

1 Classic Pieced

Lone Stars

Blazing Star

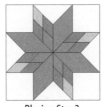

Blazing Star 2

Prairie Star

Prairie Star 2

Star of Bethlehem

Star of Bethlehem 2

Rainbow Star

Rainbow Star 2

Lone Star

Lone Star 2

Sunburst and Mills

Connecticut Star Variation

Rolling Star

Rolling Star 2

Rolling Star 3

Love in a Mist

Love in a Mist 2

Four Stars

Four Stars 2

Carpenter's Wheel

Carpenter's Wheel 2

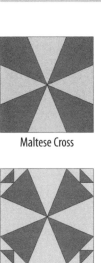

Maltese Cross

Kaleidoscope

Star of the East

Kaleidoscope Variation

Arrowheads

V Block Star

V Block

Day Lily

Key West

Spiderweb Maltese 2

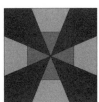

Double Maltese 2

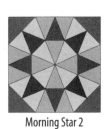

Morning Star 2

Spiderweb Maltese 3

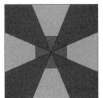

Double Maltese 3

Double Maltese 3
Variation

Morning Star 3

Spiderweb Maltese 4

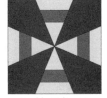

Double Maltese 4
Variation

Double Maltese 4

Morning Star 4

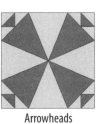
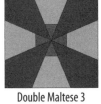

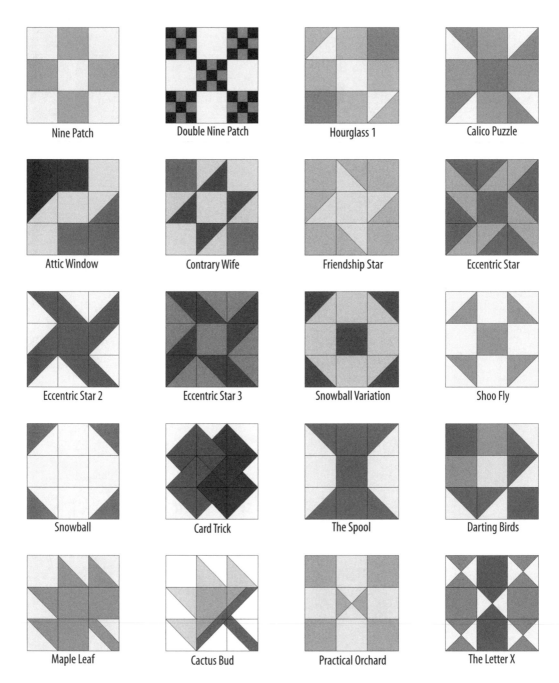

Nine Patch

Double Nine Patch

Hourglass 1

Calico Puzzle

Attic Window

Contrary Wife

Friendship Star

Eccentric Star

Eccentric Star 2

Eccentric Star 3

Snowball Variation

Shoo Fly

Snowball

Card Trick

The Spool

Darting Birds

Maple Leaf

Cactus Bud

Practical Orchard

The Letter X

Clown's Choice

Aunt Malvernia's Chain Variation

Arkansas Snowflake

Time & Tide

Mississippi

Nine-Patch Variation

Nine-Patch 2 Variation

Pinwheel Variation

Beggar Block

Optical Illusion

Arkansas Snowflake

Rolling Stone

Broken Wheel

Road to California

Rolling Squares

Kansas Star

All Hallows

Wyoming Valley

Bird of Paradise

Stellie

Mollie's Choice

Joseph's Coat

Summer Winds

Double Monkey Wrench

Classic Pieced   **41**

Grecian Square

Greek Cross

Aunt Dinah

Saw Tooth

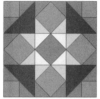

Five Spot

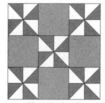

The Windmill

Two by Three

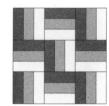

Three by Three

Four by Three

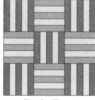

Five by Three

London Roads

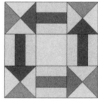

London Roads

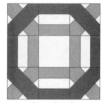

Cross Roads

1 Classic Pieced
Nine Patch Stars

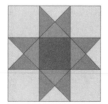

Variable Star

Aunt Eliza's Star

Rhode Island

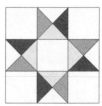

Twin Star

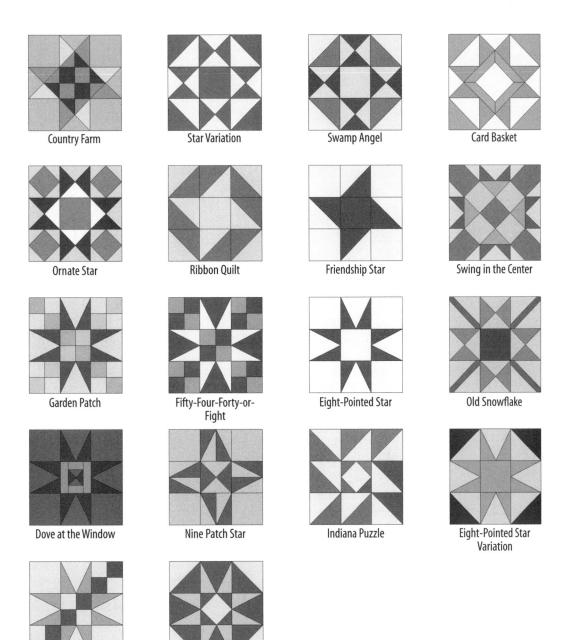

Country Farm

Star Variation

Swamp Angel

Card Basket

Ornate Star

Ribbon Quilt

Friendship Star

Swing in the Center

Garden Patch

Fifty-Four-Forty-or-Fight

Eight-Pointed Star

Old Snowflake

Dove at the Window

Nine Patch Star

Indiana Puzzle

Eight-Pointed Star Variation

Garden Patch Variation

Doris' Delight

Jewel Star

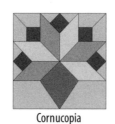
Cornucopia

Storm at Sea

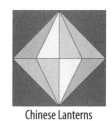
Chinese Lanterns

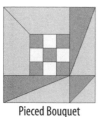
Pieced Bouquet

Nose-Gay

Silver Maple

Starry Path

Road to Fortune

Lucky Star

Full Blown Tulip

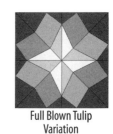
Full Blown Tulip
Variation

Pineapple

The Palm

Lotus Block

Meadow Flower

Friendship Bouquet

Whirligig

Double Windmill

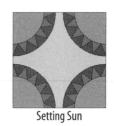
Setting Sun

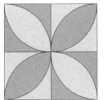

Flower Petals

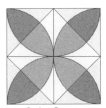

Spring Beauty

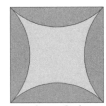

Orange Peel

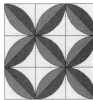

Orange Peel Variation

Sugar Bowl

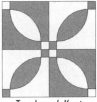

True Lover's Knot

Flowering Snowball

Papa's Delight

Raleigh

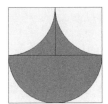

Clamshell

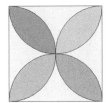

Joseph's Coat

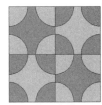

Snowball

Melon Patch

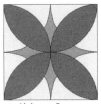

Alabama Beauty

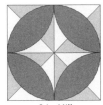

Grist Mill

Four Leaf Clover

Friendship Circle

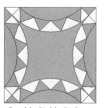

Double Pickle Dish - 4
Points

Double Pickle Dish
Side - 4 Points

Plain Double Wedding
Ring

Plain Double Wedding
Ring Side

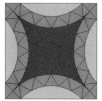

Double Pickle Dish - 5
Points

Double Pickle Dish
Side - 5 Points

Double Wedding
Ring - 4 Segments

Double Wedding Ring
Side - 4 Segments

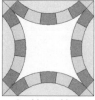

Double Wedding
Ring - 5 Segments

Double Wedding Ring
Side - 5 Segments

Double Pickle Dish - 7
Points

Double Pickle Dish
Side - 7 Points

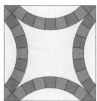

Double Wedding
Ring - 7 Segments

Double Wedding Ring
Side - 7 Segments

Plain Wedding Ring

Wedding Ring - 4
Segments

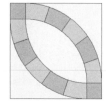

Wedding Ring - 5
Segments

Wedding Ring - 7
Segments

Pickle Dish - 4 Points

Pickle Dish - 5 Points

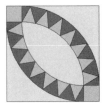

Pickle Dish - 7 Points

1 Classic Pieced
Pictures

Sunflowers

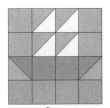

Sailboat Quilt

Boat

Airways

The Airplane

Jack's House

The Old Homestead

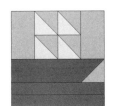

House on the Hill

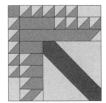

Proud Pine

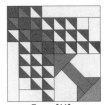

Tree of Life

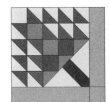

Pine Tree

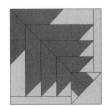

Pine Tree Quilt

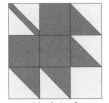

Maple Leaf

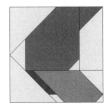

The Butterfly Quilt (2)

Butterfly

Grape Basket

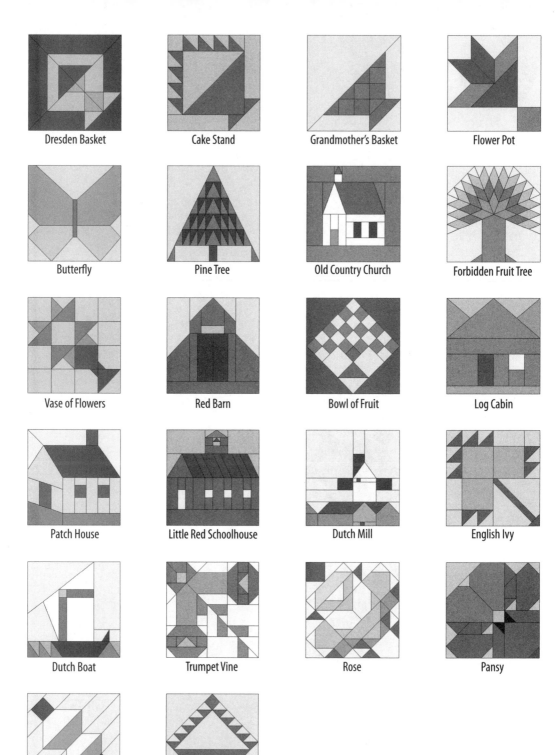

Dresden Basket

Cake Stand

Grandmother's Basket

Flower Pot

Butterfly

Pine Tree

Old Country Church

Forbidden Fruit Tree

Vase of Flowers

Red Barn

Bowl of Fruit

Log Cabin

Patch House

Little Red Schoolhouse

Dutch Mill

English Ivy

Dutch Boat

Trumpet Vine

Rose

Pansy

Lantern

Fruit Basket

Priscilla

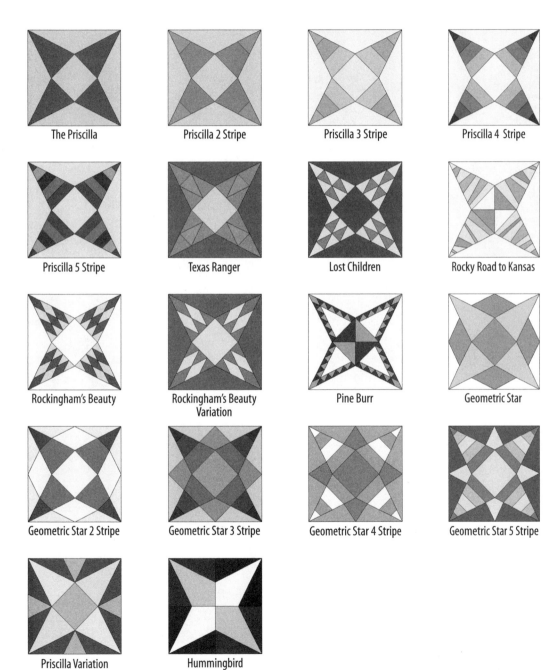

The Priscilla

Priscilla 2 Stripe

Priscilla 3 Stripe

Priscilla 4 Stripe

Priscilla 5 Stripe

Texas Ranger

Lost Children

Rocky Road to Kansas

Rockingham's Beauty

Rockingham's Beauty Variation

Pine Burr

Geometric Star

Geometric Star 2 Stripe

Geometric Star 3 Stripe

Geometric Star 4 Stripe

Geometric Star 5 Stripe

Priscilla Variation

Hummingbird

1 Classic Pieced
Simple Blocks

Half-Square Triangle

Half-Square Triangle 2

Four X

Diagonal Strips

Diagonal Strips 2

Four Patch

Four-Patch Variation

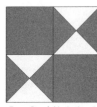
Four-Patch Variation 2

Four-Patch Variation 3

Indian Hatchets

Indian Hatchets 2

Nine Patch

Eccentric Star

Shoo Fly

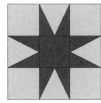
Eight-Pointed Star

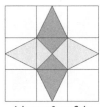
Arkansas Snowflake

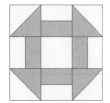
Double Monkey Wrench

The Spool

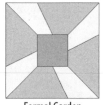
Formal Garden Variation

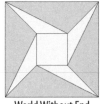
World Without End Variation

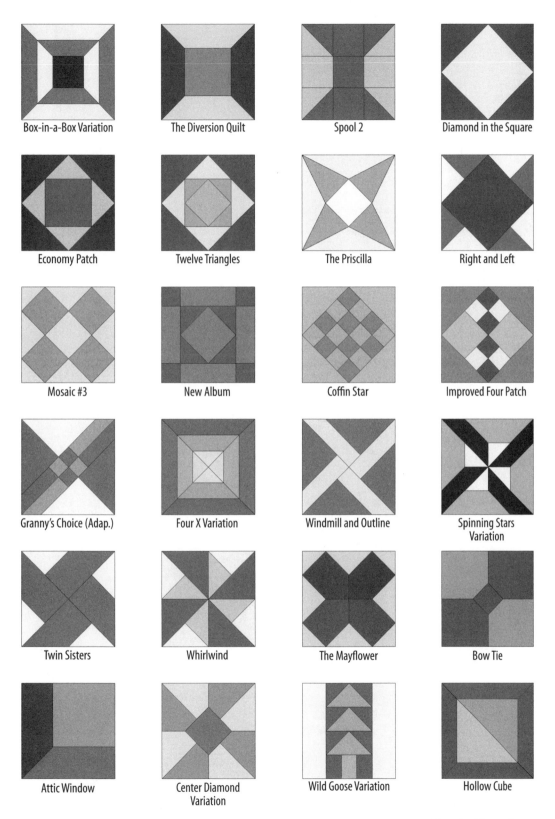

Box-in-a-Box Variation

The Diversion Quilt

Spool 2

Diamond in the Square

Economy Patch

Twelve Triangles

The Priscilla

Right and Left

Mosaic #3

New Album

Coffin Star

Improved Four Patch

Granny's Choice (Adap.)

Four X Variation

Windmill and Outline

Spinning Stars
Variation

Twin Sisters

Whirlwind

The Mayflower

Bow Tie

Attic Window

Center Diamond
Variation

Wild Goose Variation

Hollow Cube

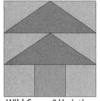

Wild Goose 2 Variation

Wild Goose Chase

Wild Goose Chase

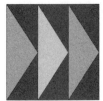

Wild Goose Chase

Wild Goose Chase

1 Classic Pieced

Stars

Double Star Variation

Little Rock Block

Square and a Half

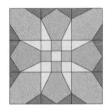

Klondike Star

Chicago Star

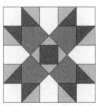

Providence Quilt Block

Uncle Sam's Hourglass

Star Variation

Star Variation

Split 12 Point Star

12 Point Star

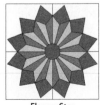

Flower Star

Rolling Plate

Fan Flower

Purple Coneflower

Sunbeam

Sunbeam Variation

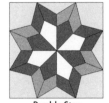

Double Star

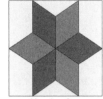

Morning Star

1 Classic Pieced
Variable Stars

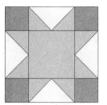

Sawtooth Star

Variable Star

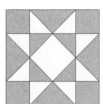

Variable Star

Sawtooth 16 Patch

Mosaic #19

Variable Star Variation

Frayed Sawtooth Star

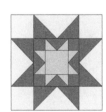

Rising Star

Eight Hands Around

Aunt Addie's Album

Sarah's Choice

Star & Pinwheels

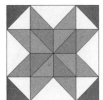

Star Puzzle

Martha Washington's
Star

Odd Fellows Chain

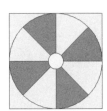

Odd Fellows Chain
Variation

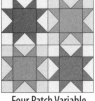

Four Patch Variable
Stars

Cats and Mice

1 Classic Pieced
Wheels

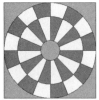

Wheel of Fortune

Wheel of Fortune

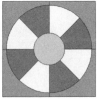

Bird's Eye View

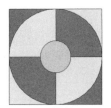

Round Table

Wagon Wheel

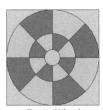

Chariot Wheel

Four Patch Circle

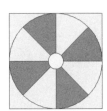

Four Blades

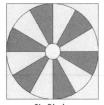

Six Blades

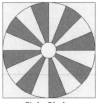

Eight Blades

Ten Blades

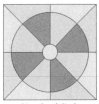

Pinwheel Circle

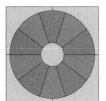

Baby Aster

Wheel of Chance

Transparent Circle

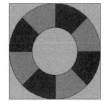

Jelly Donut

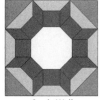

Castle Wall

Split Four Patch Circle

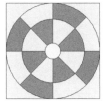

Split Four Blades

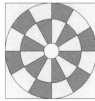

Split Six Blades

Split Eight Blades

Split Ten Blades

1 Classic Pieced

Whole Top Designs

Gameboard Medallion

Clustered Square Medallion

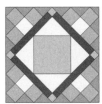

Square-in-Diamond

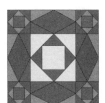

Storm at Sea

Sashed Medallion

Rick Rack Medallion

Sawtooth Medallion

Checkerboard Medallion

Small Dahlia

Giant Dahlia

Brick Path Medallion

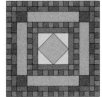

Five Border Medallion

Criss-Cross Medallion

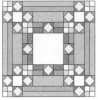

Diamonds in Squares

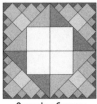

Opposing Corners

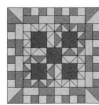

Five Stars

2 Contemporary Pieced

Autograph Block Variations 58

Baskets (Contemporary) 59

Cross Variations... 60

Fans.. 61

Fauna 63

Flora 64

Good Alternative Blocks... 65

Good for Stacking 66

Home Delights 67

Houses.. 68

Kaleidoscopes 70

Log Cabin-Like 71

New Stars 72

Pinwheels & Potpourri 73

Prairie Style 75

Royal Crowns 76

Secondary Surprises 77

Spinning Suns 78

Strip Quilts... 79

Sun Compasses 80

The Shirts 81

Trees.. 82

US Flags 83

World Flags... 84

Log Cabin Autograph

Ribbon Autograph

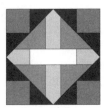

Cross with Cross Autograph

Texas Flower Autograph

January Autograph

February Autograph

March Autograph

April Autograph

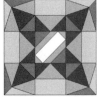

May Autograph

June Autograph

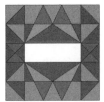

July Autograph

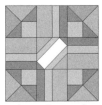

August Autograph

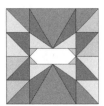

September Autograph

October Autograph

November Autograph

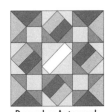

December Autograph

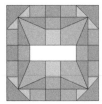

Monday Autograph

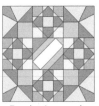

Tuesday Autograph

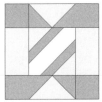

Wednesday Autograph

Thursday Autograph

Brittany Basket

Double-Baskets

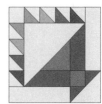

Standing Basket

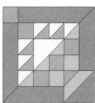

Almost Amish Basket

Easter Basket

Topiary

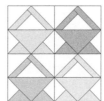

Barbershop Baskets

Checkerboard Basket

Basket Pinwheel

Postmodern Basket

Woven Basket

Berry Basket

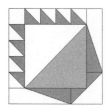

Scrap Basket

Sun & Shadow Basket

Lily Basket

Amish Basket

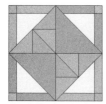

Sun & Shadow Baskets

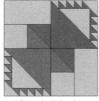

Adirondack Baskets

Sugar Creek Basket

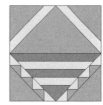

Rick-Rack Basket

Log Cabin Basket

Charm Basket

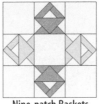

Nine-patch Baskets

Megan's Baskets

Berry Basket

2 Contemporary Pieced

Cross Variations

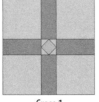

Cross 1

Cross 2

Cross 3

Cross 4

Cross 5

Cross 6

Cross 7

Cross 8

Cross 9

Cross 10

Cross 11

Cross 12

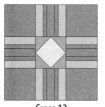

Cross 13

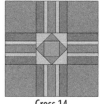

Cross 14

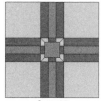

Cross 15

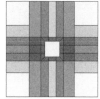

Cross 16

2 Contemporary Pieced
Fans

Fan

Sawtooth Fan

Rising Sun

Overlapping Fan

Rainbow Fan

Harvest Sun

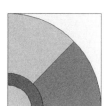

Fan Dance 2

Fan Dance 3

Fan Dance 4

Fan Dance 5

Fan Dance 6

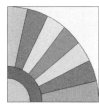

Fan Dance 7

Fan Dance 8

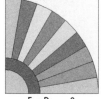

Fan Dance 9

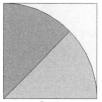

Fan 2

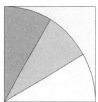

Fan 3

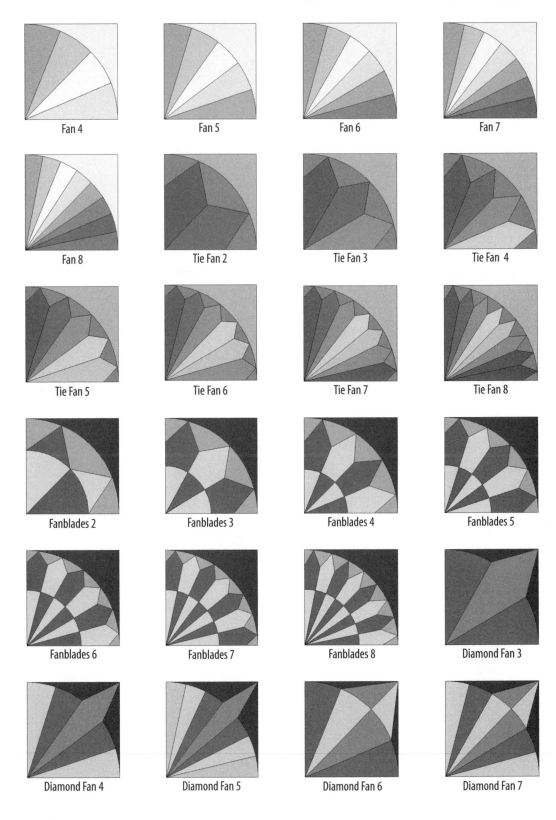

Fan 4

Fan 5

Fan 6

Fan 7

Fan 8

Tie Fan 2

Tie Fan 3

Tie Fan 4

Tie Fan 5

Tie Fan 6

Tie Fan 7

Tie Fan 8

Fanblades 2

Fanblades 3

Fanblades 4

Fanblades 5

Fanblades 6

Fanblades 7

Fanblades 8

Diamond Fan 3

Diamond Fan 4

Diamond Fan 5

Diamond Fan 6

Diamond Fan 7

Diamond Fan 8

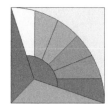

Floating Fan

Diamond Diane's Fan

Leaf Fan

North Baltimore Fan

Louvre Fan

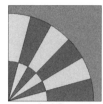

Jan's Fan

Petal Fan

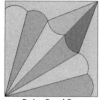

Daisy Petal Fan

Fan Flower

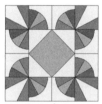

Butterfly Fan

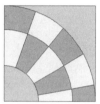

Fat Quarters Fan

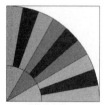

Silk Rainbow

2 Contemporary Pieced

Fauna

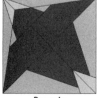

Penguin

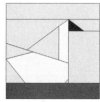

Swan

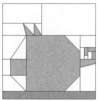

Pig

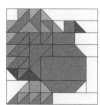

Turkey

Crab

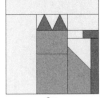

Cat

Collie

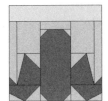

Frog Went A Courtin'

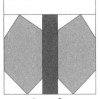

Butterfly

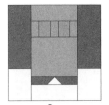

Pup

Red Fox

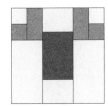

Reindeer

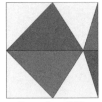

Queen Angel Fish

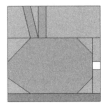

Bunny

Maine Lobster

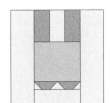

Rabbit

Polywogs

Horse

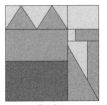

Fat Cat

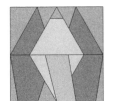

Elephant

2 Contemporary Pieced

Flora

Buds and Ribbons

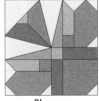

Blossom

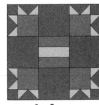

Sunflower

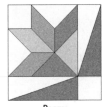

Peony

Amaryllis Bulb

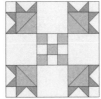

Picnic Bouquet

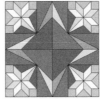

Daffodil Ring

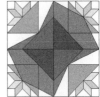

Alpine Flower

Floral Wreath

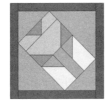

Rosebud

Rose

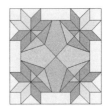

Foxglove

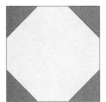

Foxglove Too

Tulip

Lily Block

Lily Wreath

2 Contemporary Pieced

Good Alternative Blocks

9-Patch Snowball

4-Patch Snowball

Rail Fence Quilt

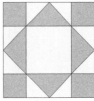

9-Patch

Chain 1

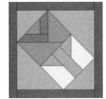

9-Patch Chain

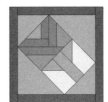

4-Patch Chain

Economy

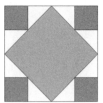

Economy 2

Cross X

Uneven Cross X

Wide Cross X

Broken Sash Strip

Broken Sash Strip 2

Broken Sash Strip 3

Puss in the Corner

Half-Square Triangle

Four X

2 Contemporary Pieced

Good for Stacking

LeMoyne Star

Grandmother's Fan

Twin Sisters

Quarter-Square
Triangles

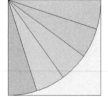

Fan 5

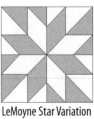

LeMoyne Star Variation

Wild Goose Chase

Electric Fan

Windmill

Windmill

Pinwheel

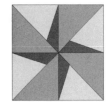

Double Pinwheel
Whirls

Square Dance

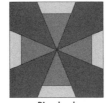

Pinwheel

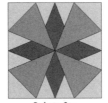

Dakota Star

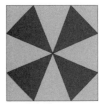

Kaleidoscope

2 Contemporary Pieced

Home Delights

EQ Logo

Bathtub Boat

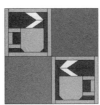

Hot Latte

Birthday Party

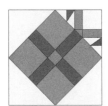

Happy Returns

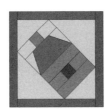

Bird House

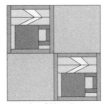

Good Morning

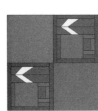

Good Night

He

She

Toy Barn

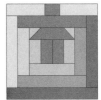

Log Cabin Doll

She and He (Judy Vigiletti)

Two Friends (Judy Vigiletti)

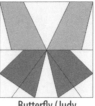

Butterfly (Judy Vigiletti)

Butterfly Too (Judy Vigiletti)

Fish (Judy Vigiletti)

Fish Too (Judy Vigiletti)

Fish Too 2 (Judy Vigiletti)

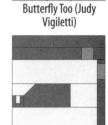

Sewing Machine

Fabric Bolts

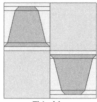

Thimbles

Star of David (Debbie Sichel)

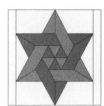

Star of David 2 (Debbie Sichel)

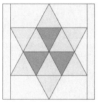

Star of David 3 (Debbie Sichel)

Star of David 4 (Debbie Sichel)

2 Contemporary Pieced

Houses

Log Cabin

Log Cabin 2

Little Red Schoolhouse

Country Cottage

Brooklyn

St. Louis

Bowling Green

Chicago

Baltimore

Milwaukee

Philadelphia

Detroit

Kansas City

Saltbox

Lighthouse

Prairie House

Picket Fence

Terrie's in Taos

Condo

Wisconsin Cabin

The Lake Cottage

Old Two-Story

Ann's House

Schoolhouse

Honeymoon Cottage

Log Cabin

Early Colonial Cottage

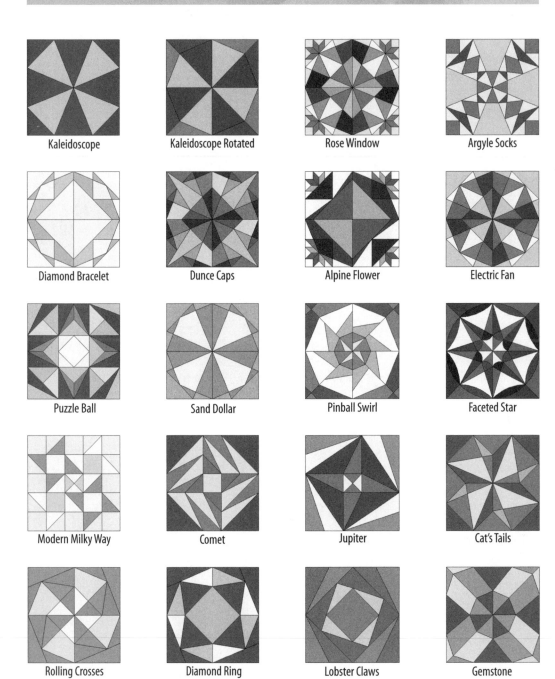

Kaleidoscope

Kaleidoscope Rotated

Rose Window

Argyle Socks

Diamond Bracelet

Dunce Caps

Alpine Flower

Electric Fan

Puzzle Ball

Sand Dollar

Pinball Swirl

Faceted Star

Modern Milky Way

Comet

Jupiter

Cat's Tails

Rolling Crosses

Diamond Ring

Lobster Claws

Gemstone

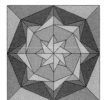

Star Flower

Snowflake 1

Snowflake 2

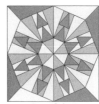

Snowflake 3

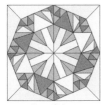

Snowflake 4

2 Contemporary Pieced

Log Cabin-Like

Courthouse Stars

Rotary Ribbon

Strip Circles

Fan Rails

Round Cabin

Scrappy Stripper

Rainbow Logs

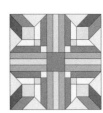

Starflower

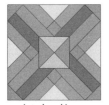

Interlaced Logs

Irish Logs

Floating Pinwheels

Lacy Lattice Work

Striped Lattice Work

3's

7's

High Flying Squares

Plaid Lattice

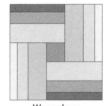
Woven Logs

Plaid Fab

2 Contemporary Pieced

New Stars

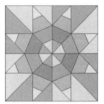
String Star

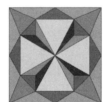
Hopatcong Star

Shadow Star

Sedona Star

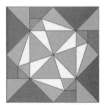
Mule Shoe TX

Bettina's Star

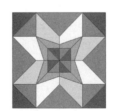
Cheyenne Star

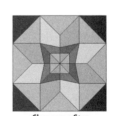
Cheyenne Star
Variation

Folded Star

Strip Star

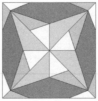
Propeller

Savannah Star

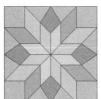
EQ's Stars & Beams

Stars & Beams
Variation

Sara's Star

Sara's Star Variation

Lu's Star

Lu's Star Variation

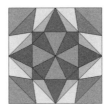
EQ Kaleidoscope Star

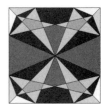
Fireworks Star

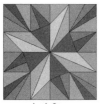
Jan's Star

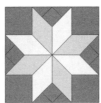
Diamond Star

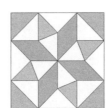
EQ Star

EQ Star 2

EQ Star 3

EQ Star 4

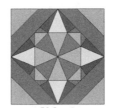
EQ Star 5

EQ Star 6

2 Contemporary Pieced
Pinwheels & Potpourri

Woven Lattice

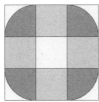
Button

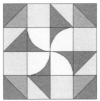
Electric Fan

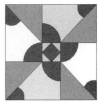
Scrap Blossoms

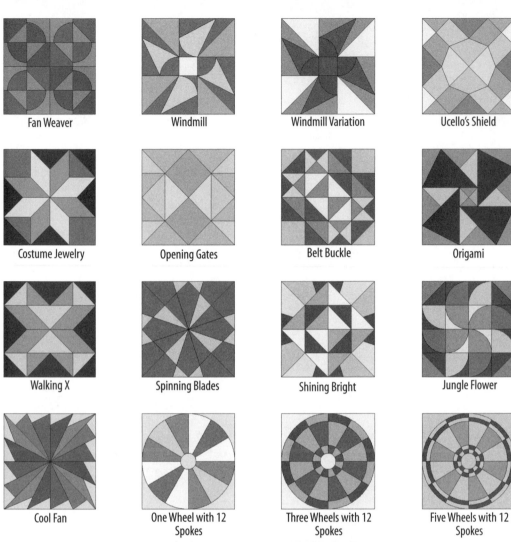

Fan Weaver

Windmill

Windmill Variation

Ucello's Shield

Costume Jewelry

Opening Gates

Belt Buckle

Origami

Walking X

Spinning Blades

Shining Bright

Jungle Flower

Cool Fan

One Wheel with 12
Spokes

Three Wheels with 12
Spokes

Five Wheels with 12
Spokes

Nine Degree Wedge

Perspective Grid 1

Perspective Grid 2

Prairie Style

Bel Geddes

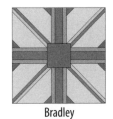

Bradley

Burnham

Downing

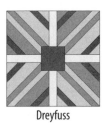

Dreyfuss

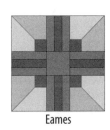

Eames

Eastlake

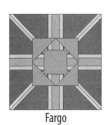

Fargo

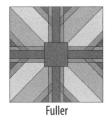

Fuller

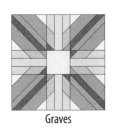

Graves

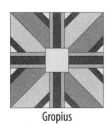

Gropius

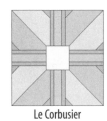

Le Corbusier

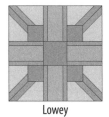

Lowey

Roche

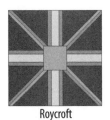

Roycroft

Stickley

Sullivan

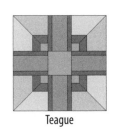

Teague

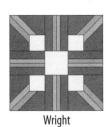

Wright

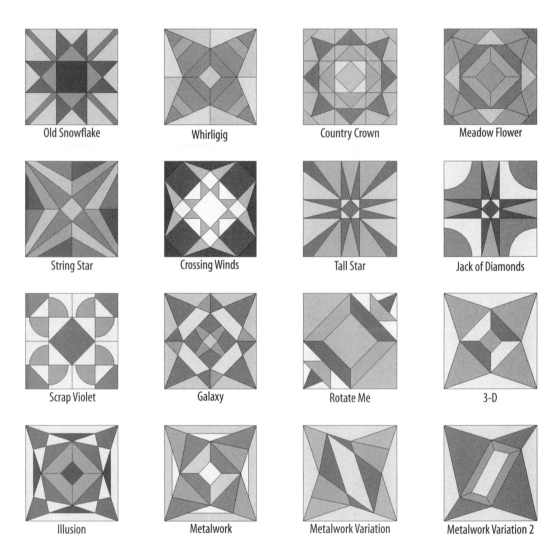

Old Snowflake

Whirligig

Country Crown

Meadow Flower

String Star

Crossing Winds

Tall Star

Jack of Diamonds

Scrap Violet

Galaxy

Rotate Me

3-D

Illusion

Metalwork

Metalwork Variation

Metalwork Variation 2

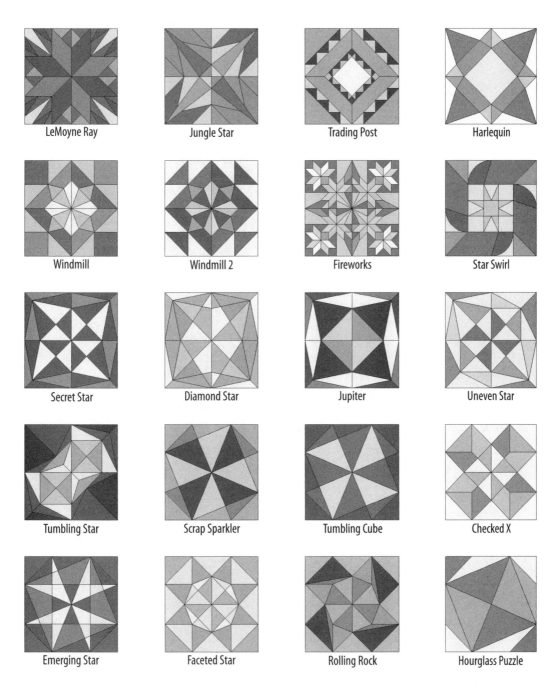

LeMoyne Ray

Jungle Star

Trading Post

Harlequin

Windmill

Windmill 2

Fireworks

Star Swirl

Secret Star

Diamond Star

Jupiter

Uneven Star

Tumbling Star

Scrap Sparkler

Tumbling Cube

Checked X

Emerging Star

Faceted Star

Rolling Rock

Hourglass Puzzle

LeMoyne Ray Split

2 Contemporary Pieced

Spinning Suns

Black-Eyed Susan

Sun Spin

Star Dahlia

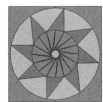

Kirsten's Star

Diamond Diane

September Flower

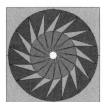

Nevada Star

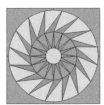

Rhode Island Star

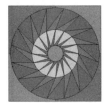

Hawaii Star

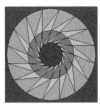

Dizzy Spinner

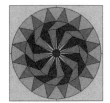

Blueberry Pie

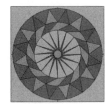

Rhubarb Pie

Key Lime Pie

Raspberry Cream

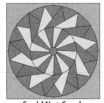

Cool Mint Candy

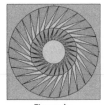

Fireworks

2 Contemporary Pieced
Strip Quilts

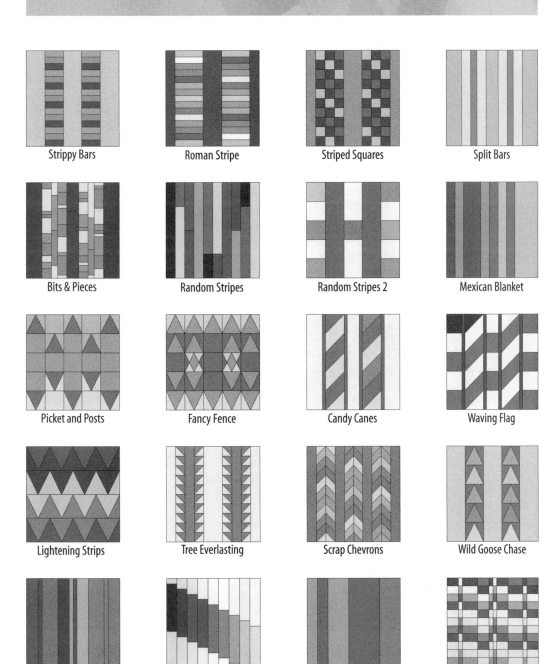

Strippy Bars	Roman Stripe	Striped Squares	Split Bars
Bits & Pieces	Random Stripes	Random Stripes 2	Mexican Blanket
Picket and Posts	Fancy Fence	Candy Canes	Waving Flag
Lightening Strips	Tree Everlasting	Scrap Chevrons	Wild Goose Chase
Andrea's Blanket	Rainbow Steps	Random Stripes 2	Simple Bargello

Dean's Sunflower Sun

Diamond Sun

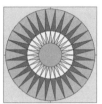

Sun Spokes

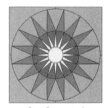

Sun Spokes 2

Sun Compass 1

Sun Compass 2

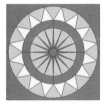

Monkey Overboard Compass

Sun Compass 3

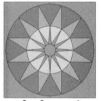

Sun Compass 4

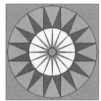

Sun Circle

Prairie Point Sun

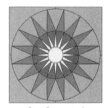

Sun Wheel 1

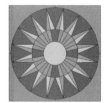

Sun Wheel 2

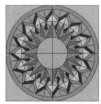

Northern Lights Compass

Star within Sun

South Pole Star

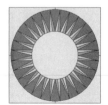

August Sun

Sun Swirl

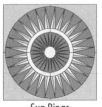

Sun Rings

Sun Rings 2

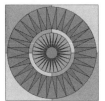

Sun Rings 3

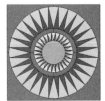

Sun Rings 4

Sedona's Sun

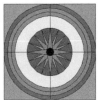

Hazel Eye Compass

2 Contemporary Pieced

The Shirts

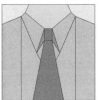

Blue Shirt

Shirt & Sweater

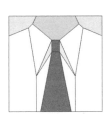

Starched Shirt

Work Shirt

Suspenders

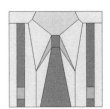

Executive

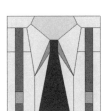

The Harvard Club

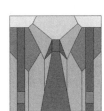

Country Lawyer

T-Shirt

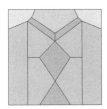

Logo T-Shirt

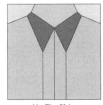

No Tie Shirt

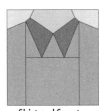

Shirt and Sweater

Stuffed Shirt

Bored Meeting

Cowboy Shirt

Pocket Protecter

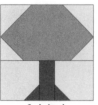
Crab Apple

Big & Little Trees

Sweet Gum

Snowy Pine

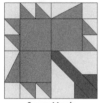
Sugar Maple

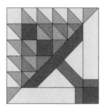
Hemlock

Pinwheel Pine

Christmas Pine

Mulberry Bush

Blue Spruce

Birds in the Pine

Log Cabin Tree

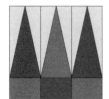
Topiary Trio

Topiary Trio Too

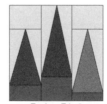
Topiary Trio 3

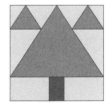
Big Pine

Evergreen

Three Trees

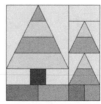
Striped Big & Little

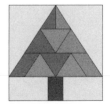
Triangle Tree

Triangle Tree 2

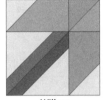
Tree in the Forest

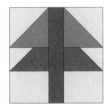
Red Maple

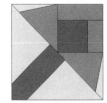
Diamond-in-the-Tree

Geometric Tree

Willow

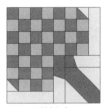
Blue Spruce

Blue Spruce 2

Umbrella Tree

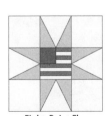
Tree on a Hill

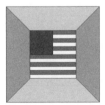
Old Oak

2 Contemporary Pieced

US Flags

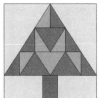
United States

Eight-Point Flag

Flag in a Box

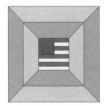
Flag in a Box 2

Attic Flag

Flag in the Square

Wild Goose Flag

Wild Goose Flag 2

Heart Flag

Heart Flag 2

Log Cabin Flag

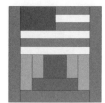

Log Cabin Flag 2

Log Cabin Flag 3

Lady of the Lake Flag

Whirlwind Flag

Rail Fence Flag

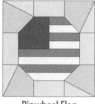

Pinwheel Flag

2 Contemporary Pieced

World Flags

Algeria

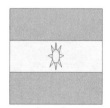

Argentina

Armenia

Australia

Austria

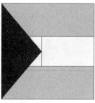

The Bahamas

Barbados

Belgium

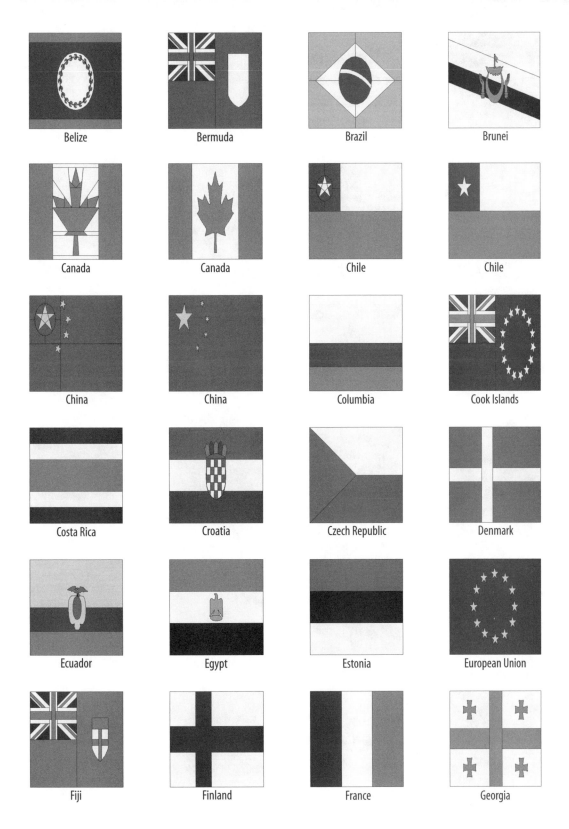

| Belize | Bermuda | Brazil | Brunei |

| Canada | Canada | Chile | Chile |

| China | China | Columbia | Cook Islands |

| Costa Rica | Croatia | Czech Republic | Denmark |

| Ecuador | Egypt | Estonia | European Union |

| Fiji | Finland | France | Georgia |

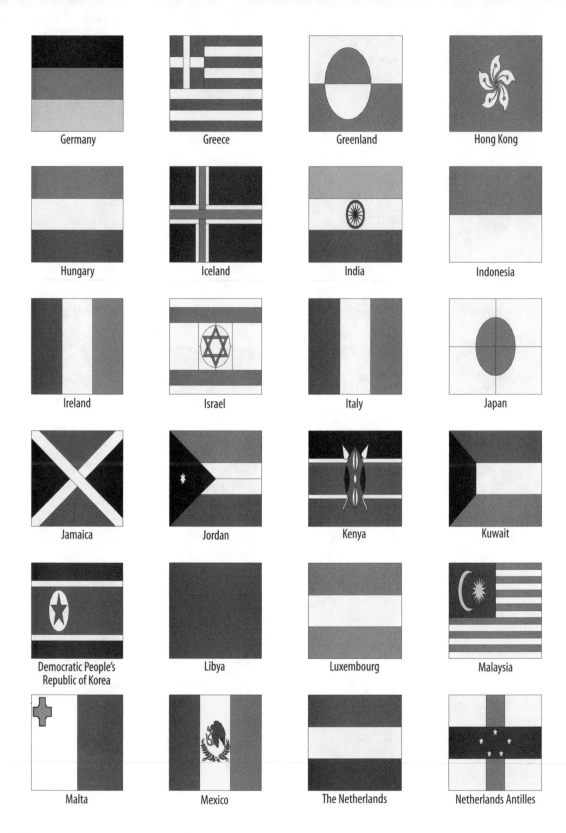

Germany

Greece

Greenland

Hong Kong

Hungary

Iceland

India

Indonesia

Ireland

Israel

Italy

Japan

Jamaica

Jordan

Kenya

Kuwait

Democratic People's
Republic of Korea

Libya

Luxembourg

Malaysia

Malta

Mexico

The Netherlands

Netherlands Antilles

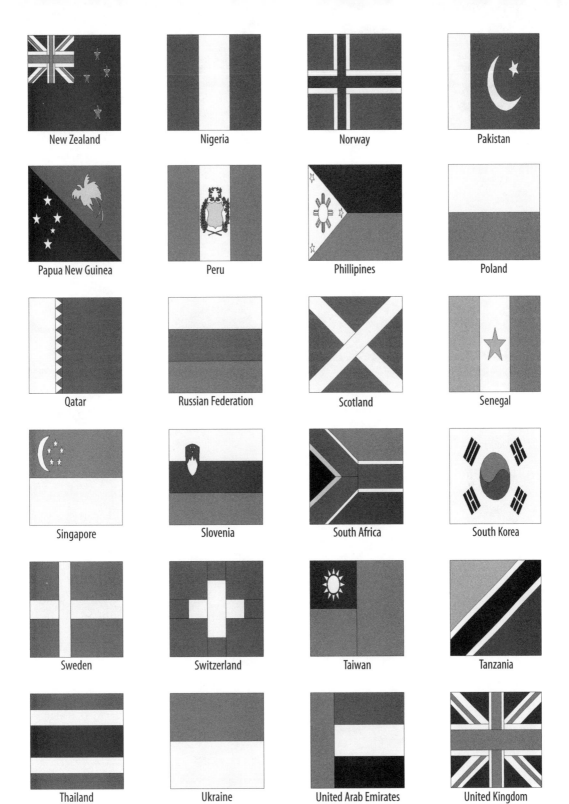

New Zealand

Nigeria

Norway

Pakistan

Papua New Guinea

Peru

Phillipines

Poland

Qatar

Russian Federation

Scotland

Senegal

Singapore

Slovenia

South Africa

South Korea

Sweden

Switzerland

Taiwan

Tanzania

Thailand

Ukraine

United Arab Emirates

United Kingdom

Venezuela

3 Foundation Pieced

Alphabet - Greek 90

Alphabet - Hebrew© 92

Alphabet - Standard 93

Animals 97

Baskets 98

Beach Panorama 99

Cars and Trucks 100

Celebrations 101

Crazy Blocks - Complex 102

Crazy Blocks - Simple 103

Flowerbed Foundations 104

Flowers 106

Flying Geese 107

Fruits and Vegetables 108

Fun Stuff 109

Geometrics 110

Holiday Foundations 111

Houses 113

In the Woods 114

Log Cabins 115

New York Beauties 117

Pineapples 118

Stained Glass Blocks 119

Stained Glass Pictures 121

Stained Glass Quarters 122

Toys 123

Trees 124

Twists 125

Alpha (Greek Alphabet)

alpha (Greek Alphabet)

Beta (Greek Alphabet)

beta (Greek Alphabet)

Gamma (Greek Alphabet)

gamma (Greek Alphabet)

Delta (Greek Alphabet)

delta (Greek Alphabet)

Epsilon (Greek Alphabet)

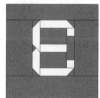

epsilon (Greek Alphabet)

Zeta (Greek Alphabet)

zeta (Greek Alphabet)

Eta (Greek Alphabet)

eta (Greek Alphabet)

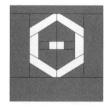

Theta (Greek Alphabet)

theta (Greek Alphabet)

Iota (Greek Alphabet)

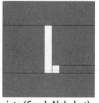

iota (Greek Alphabet)

Kappa (Greek Alphabet)

kappa (Greek Alphabet)

Lamda (Greek Alphabet)

lamda (Greek Alphabet)

Mu (Greek Alphabet)

mu (Greek Alphabet)

Nu (Greek Alphabet)

nu (Greek Alphabet)

Xi (Greek Alphabet)

xi (Greek Alphabet)

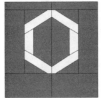

Omicron (Greek Alphabet)

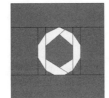

omicron (Greek Alphabet)

Pi (Greek Alphabet)

pi (Greek Alphabet)

Rho (Greek Alphabet)

rho (Greek Alphabet)

Sigma (Greek Alphabet)

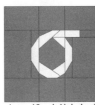

sigma (Greek Alphabet)

final sigma (Greek Alphabet)

Tau (Greek Alphabet)

tau (Greek Alphabet)

Upsilon (Greek Alphabet)

upsilon (Greek Alphabet)

Phi (Greek Alphabet)

phi (Greek Alphabet)

Chi (Greek Alphabet)

chi (Greek Alphabet)

Psi (Greek Alphabet)

psi (Greek Alphabet)

Omega (Greek Alphabet)

omega (Greek Alphabet)

3 Foundation Pieced
Alphabet - Hebrew©

Aleph © Debbie Sichel

Bet © Debbie Sichel

Gimel © Debbie Sichel

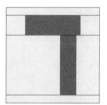

Dalet © Debbie Sichel

Hey © Debbie Sichel

Vav © Debbie Sichel

Zayin © Debbie Sichel

Chet © Debbie Sichel

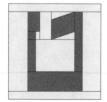

Tet © Debbie Sichel

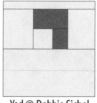

Yod © Debbie Sichel

Kaf © Debbie Sichel

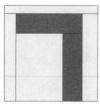

Kaf Sofeet © Debbie Sichel

Lamed © Debbie Sichel

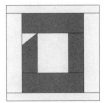

Mem © Debbie Sichel

Mem Sofeet © Debbie Sichel

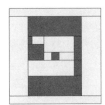

Nun © Debbie Sichel

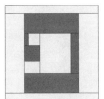

Nun Sofeet © Debbie Sichel

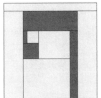

Samech © Debbie Sichel

Ayin © Debbie Sichel

Peh © Debbie Sichel

Feh © Debbie Sichel

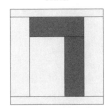

Feh Sofeet © Debbie Sichel

Tsadi © Debbie Sichel

Tsadi Sofeet © Debbie Sichel

Qof © Debbie Sichel

Resh © Debbie Sichel

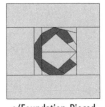

Shin © Debbie Sichel

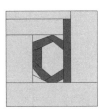

Tav © Debbie Sichel

3 Foundation Pieced

Alphabet - Standard

a (Foundation-Pieced Alphabet)

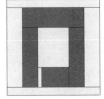

b (Foundation-Pieced Alphabet)

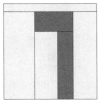

c (Foundation-Pieced Alphabet)

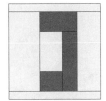

d (Foundation-Pieced Alphabet)

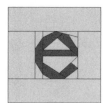

e (Foundation-Pieced Alphabet)

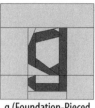

f (Foundation-Pieced Alphabet)

g (Foundation-Pieced Alphabet)

h (Foundation-Pieced Alphabet)

i (Foundation-Pieced Alphabet)

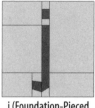

j (Foundation-Pieced Alphabet)

k (Foundation-Pieced Alphabet)

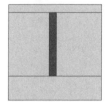

l (Foundation-Pieced Alphabet)

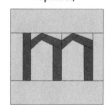

m (Foundation-Pieced Alphabet)

n (Foundation-Pieced Alphabet)

o (Foundation-Pieced Alphabet)

p (Foundation-Pieced Alphabet)

q (Foundation-Pieced Alphabet)

r (Foundation-Pieced Alphabet)

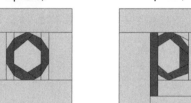

s (Foundation-Pieced Alphabet)

t (Foundation-Pieced Alphabet)

u (Foundation-Pieced Alphabet)

v (Foundation-Pieced Alphabet)

w (Foundation-Pieced Alphabet)

x (Foundation-Pieced Alphabet)

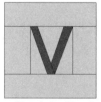

y (Foundation-Pieced Alphabet)

z (Foundation-Pieced Alphabet)

A (Foundation-Pieced Alphabet)

y (Foundation-Pieced Alphabet)

z (Foundation-Pieced Alphabet)

A (Foundation-Pieced Alphabet)

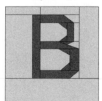

B (Foundation-Pieced Alphabet)

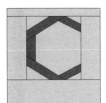

C (Foundation-Pieced
Alphabet)

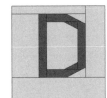

D (Foundation-Pieced
Alphabet)

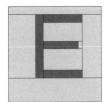

E (Foundation-Pieced
Alphabet)

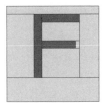

F (Foundation-Pieced
Alphabet)

G (Foundation-Pieced
Alphabet)

H (Foundation-Pieced
Alphabet)

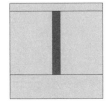

I (Foundation-Pieced
Alphabet)

J (Foundation-Pieced
Alphabet)

K (Foundation-Pieced
Alphabet)

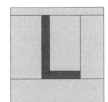

L (Foundation-Pieced
Alphabet)

M (Foundation-Pieced
Alphabet)

N (Foundation-Pieced
Alphabet)

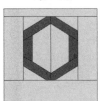

O (Foundation-Pieced
Alphabet)

P (Foundation-Pieced
Alphabet)

Q (Foundation-Pieced
Alphabet)

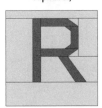

R (Foundation-Pieced
Alphabet)

S (Foundation-Pieced
Alphabet)

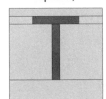

T (Foundation-Pieced
Alphabet)

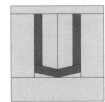

U (Foundation-Pieced
Alphabet)

V (Foundation-Pieced
Alphabet)

W (Foundation-Pieced
Alphabet)

X (Foundation-Pieced
Alphabet)

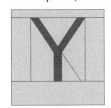

Y (Foundation-Pieced
Alphabet)

Z (Foundation-Pieced
Alphabet)

a grave (Foundation-
Pieced Alphabet)

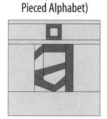

a acute (Foundation-
Pieced Alphabet)

a circumflex (Foundation-
Pieced Alphabet)

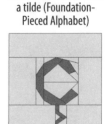

a tilde (Foundation-
Pieced Alphabet)

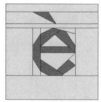

a umlaut (Foundation-
Pieced Alphabet)

a ring (Foundation-
Pieced Alphabet)

ae diphthong (Foundation-
Pieced Alphabet)

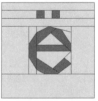

c cedilla (Foundation-
Pieced Alphabet)

e grave (Foundation-
Pieced Alphabet)

e acute (Foundation-
Pieced Alphabet)

e circumflex (Foundation-
Pieced Alphabet)

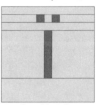

e umlaut (Foundation-
Pieced Alphabet)

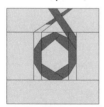

i grave (Foundation-
Pieced Alphabet)

i acute (Foundation-
Pieced Alphabet)

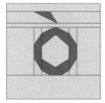

i circumflex (Foundation-
Pieced Alphabet)

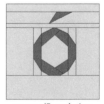

i umlaut (Foundation-
Pieced Alphabet)

eth (Foundation-Pieced
Alphabet)

n tilde (Foundation-
Pieced Alphabet)

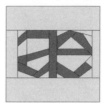

o grave (Foundation-
Pieced Alphabet)

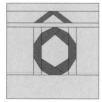

o acute (Foundation-
Pieced Alphabet)

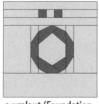

o circumflex (Foundation-
Pieced Alphabet)

o tilde (Foundation-
Pieced Alphabet)

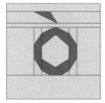

o umlaut (Foundation-
Pieced Alphabet)

o slash (Foundation-
Pieced Alphabet)

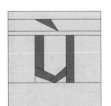

u grave (Foundation-Pieced Alphabet)

u acute (Foundation-Pieced Alphabet)

u circumflex (Foundation-Pieced Alphabet)

u umlaut (Foundation-Pieced Alphabet)

y acute (Foundation-Pieced Alphabet)

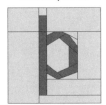

thorn (Foundation-Pieced Alphabet)

y umlaut (Foundation-Pieced Alphabet)

3 Foundation Pieced
Animals

Alligator

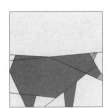

Bear

Bison

Blue Heron

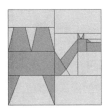

Camel

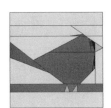

Cardinal

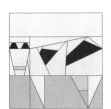

Cow

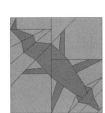

Crocodile

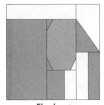

Elephant

Flamingo

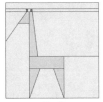

Giraffe

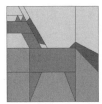

Horse

Monkey

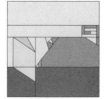

Mouse

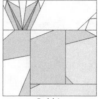

Panda

Puffin

Swan

Peacock

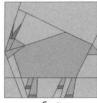

Rabbit

Goat

Rhinoceros

3 Foundation Pieced

Baskets

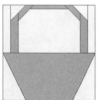

Curved-handle Basket

Striped Curved-handle
Basket

Basket with Trim

Basket

Striped Basket

On-point Basket

On-point Basket 2

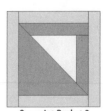

On-point Basket 3

On-point Basket 4

Basket on the Table

Bowl on Striped Cloth

Striped Bowl on Cloth

Basket

Big Basket

Big Striped Basket

On-point Layered Basket

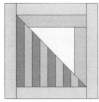

On-point Layered Basket 2

Layered Basket

Round Basket

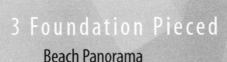

3 Foundation Pieced
Beach Panorama

Palm Tree 1

Palm Tree 2

Palm Tree 3

Motel

Sand Dune 1

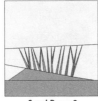

Sand Dune 2

Lifeguard Stand 1

Chair and Umbrella

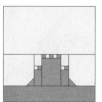
Sand Castle

Bucket and Shovel

Lifeguard Stand 2

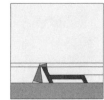
Chair and Towel

Beach 1

Beach 2

Waves

Windsurf Board

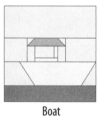
Boat

Waves and Fish

3 Foundation Pieced
Cars and Trucks

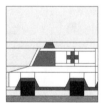
Ambulance

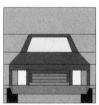
Car Front

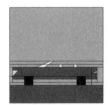
Convertible

Sedan

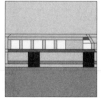
School Bus

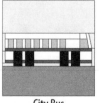
City Bus

Race Car

Sports Car

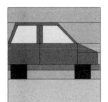

Compact Car

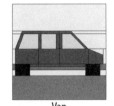

Station Wagon

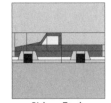

SUV

Double-Decker Bus

Fire Truck

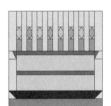

Van

Pick-up Truck

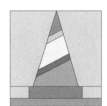

Semi Truck

3 Foundation Pieced
Celebrations

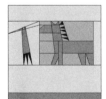

Graduation Cap

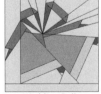

Birthday Cake

Present

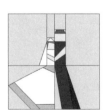

Party Hat

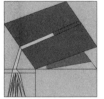

Pin the Tail on the Donkey

Wedding Bells

Two Turtle Doves

First Dance

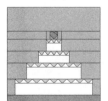

Wedding Cake

Foundation Pieced Wedding Ring

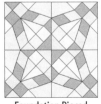

Foundation Pieced Wedding Ring 2

Foundation Pieced Wedding Ring 3

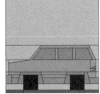

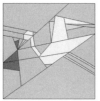

Stork and Bundle of Joy

Baby Bottle

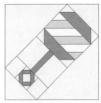

Baby Rattle

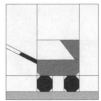

Baby Stroller

3 Foundation Pieced
Crazy Blocks - Complex

Crazy Geese 1

Crazy Geese 2

Crazy Geese 3

Crazy Geese 4

Complex Crazy 1

Complex Crazy 2

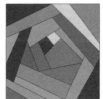

Complex Crazy 3

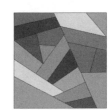

Complex Crazy 4

Complex Crazy 5

Complex Crazy 6

Complex Crazy 7

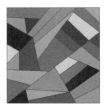

Complex Crazy 8

Complex Crazy 9

Complex Crazy 10

Complex Crazy 11

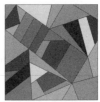

Complex Crazy 12

Complex Crazy 13

Complex Crazy 14

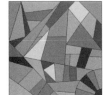

Crazy Fan 1

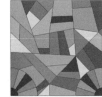

Crazy Fan 2

Crazy Fan 3

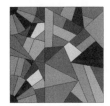

Crazy Fan 4

Crazy Fan 5

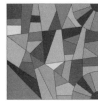

Crazy Fan 6

Crazy Fan 7

Crazy Fan 8

3 Foundation Pieced
Crazy Blocks - Simple

Crazy 1

Crazy 2

Crazy 3

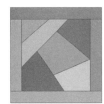

Crazy 4

Crazy 5

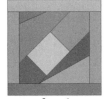

Crazy 6

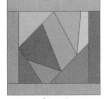

Crazy 7

Crazy 8

Crazy 9

Crazy 10

Crazy 11

Crazy 12

Crazy 13

Crazy 14

Crazy 15

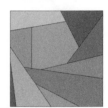

Crazy 16

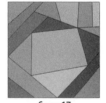

Crazy 17

Crazy 18

Crazy 19

Crazy 20

3 Foundation Pieced
Flowerbed Foundations

Potted Flowers

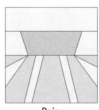

Daisy

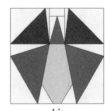

Iris

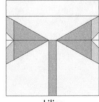

Lilies

Aster

Tulip Bud

Mum

Rose

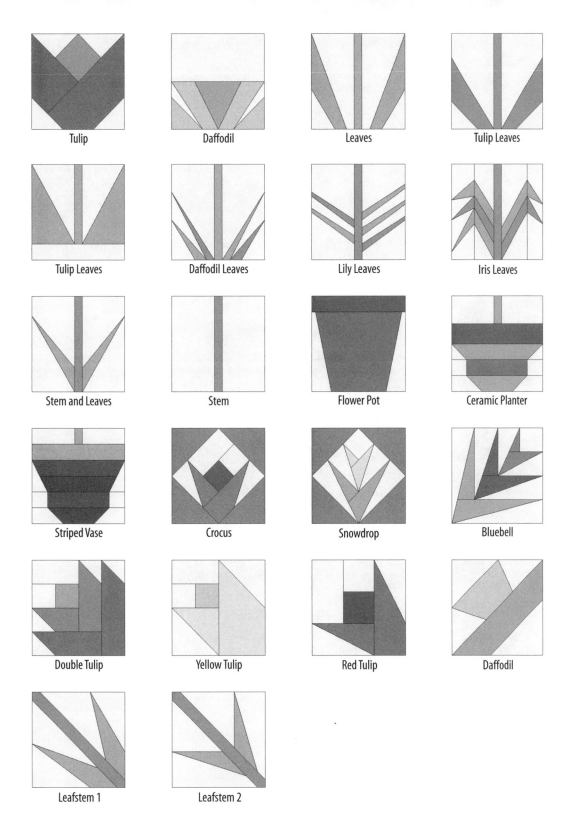

Tulip

Daffodil

Leaves

Tulip Leaves

Tulip Leaves

Daffodil Leaves

Lily Leaves

Iris Leaves

Stem and Leaves

Stem

Flower Pot

Ceramic Planter

Striped Vase

Crocus

Snowdrop

Bluebell

Double Tulip

Yellow Tulip

Red Tulip

Daffodil

Leafstem 1

Leafstem 2

3 Foundation Pieced
Flowers

Morning Glory	Aster	African Violets	Anthurium
Poppy	Bachelor's Button	Black-eyed Susan	Honeysuckle
Chrysanthemum	Primrose	Crepe Myrtle	Daffodil
Iris	Lilies	Lily	Orchid

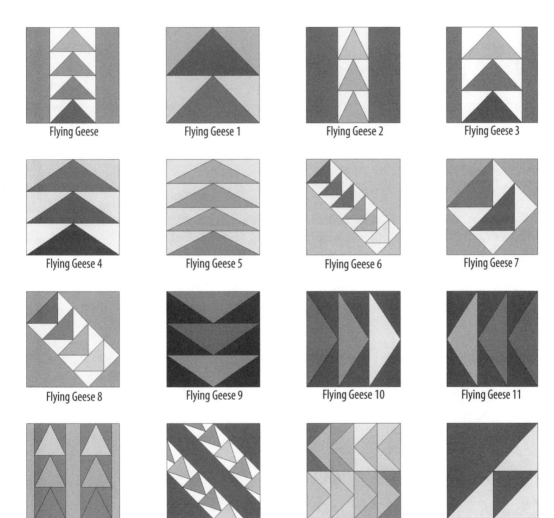

Flying Geese

Flying Geese 1

Flying Geese 2

Flying Geese 3

Flying Geese 4

Flying Geese 5

Flying Geese 6

Flying Geese 7

Flying Geese 8

Flying Geese 9

Flying Geese 10

Flying Geese 11

Flying Geese 12

Flying Geese 13

Flying Geese 14

Flying Goose

Flying Goose Variation

Apple

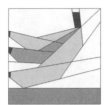

Bananas

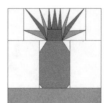

Pineapple

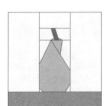

Pear

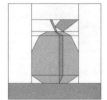

Peach

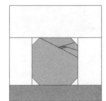

Orange

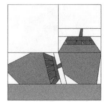

Strawberries

Tomato

Radishes

Carrot

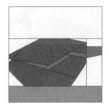

Pepper

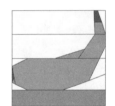

Squash

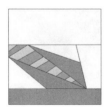

Corn

Eggplant

Asparagus

Mushrooms

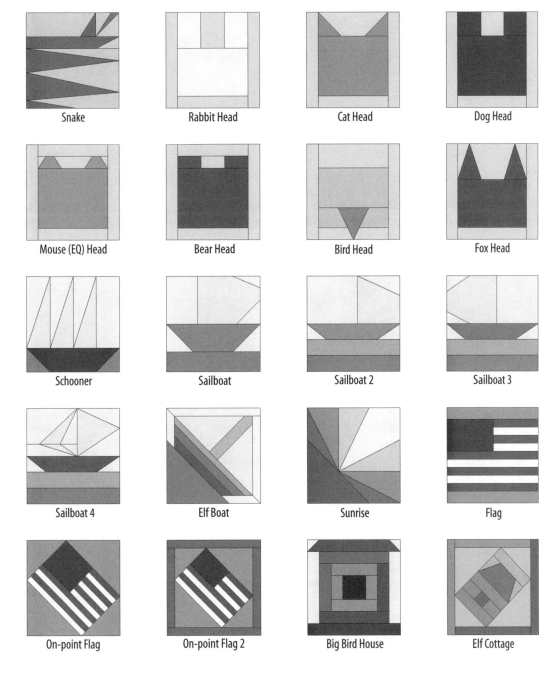

Snake	Rabbit Head	Cat Head	Dog Head
Mouse (EQ) Head	Bear Head	Bird Head	Fox Head
Schooner	Sailboat	Sailboat 2	Sailboat 3
Sailboat 4	Elf Boat	Sunrise	Flag
On-point Flag	On-point Flag 2	Big Bird House	Elf Cottage

Elf Asleep

Elf Tree

Another Elf Tree

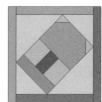

Another Tiny Tree

Tiny House

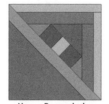

House Beneath the Bridge

Topsy-Turvy House

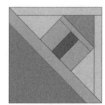

Tiny House Too

3 Foundation Pieced
Geometrics

Rail Fence

Rail Fence

Rail Fence 2

Rail Fence 3

Diagonal Strips

Diagonal Strips 2

Blocks in a Box

Blocks in a Box Variation

Blocks in a Box Variation 2

American Chain

Quarter Log Cabin

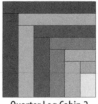

Quarter Log Cabin 2

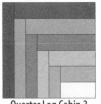

Quarter Log Cabin 3

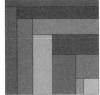

Quarter Log Cabin 4

Quarter Log Cabin 5

Quarter Log Cabin 6

Cracker

Letter H

Diamond in the Square

Economy Patch

Twelve Triangles

Album

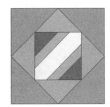

Album 2

Broken Band Variation

3 Foundation Pieced
Holiday Foundations

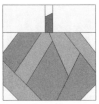

Pumpkin

Jack-O-Lantern

Witch

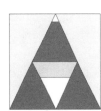

Santa

Pandora's Present

Surprise Package

Gift Box

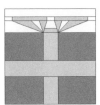

Gift with a Bow

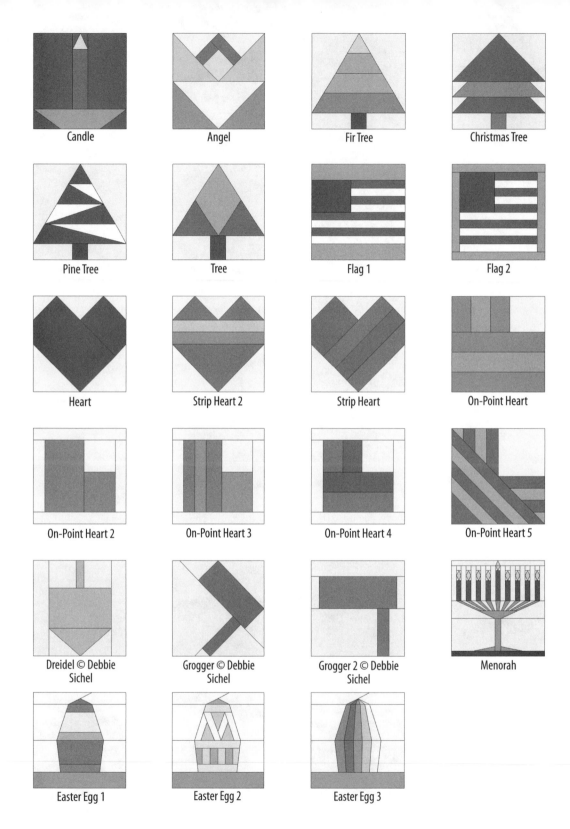

Candle

Angel

Fir Tree

Christmas Tree

Pine Tree

Tree

Flag 1

Flag 2

Heart

Strip Heart 2

Strip Heart

On-Point Heart

On-Point Heart 2

On-Point Heart 3

On-Point Heart 4

On-Point Heart 5

Dreidel © Debbie Sichel

Grogger © Debbie Sichel

Grogger 2 © Debbie Sichel

Menorah

Easter Egg 1

Easter Egg 2

Easter Egg 3

Contemporary House 1

Georgian House 1

Georgian House 2

House with Fence

Tudor Mansion

Courthouse

Townhouses 1

Split Level House

House with Porches

Contemporary House 2

Brownstones

Townhouses 2

Farm House

Southwestern House

Haunted House

McMansion

Church with Steeple

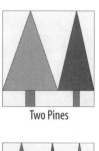

Two Pines

Sugar Maple

Deer and a Tree

Bear and a Tree

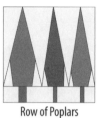

Row of Poplars

Pine

White Oak

Fir

Under the Rainbow

Little House

Log Cabin

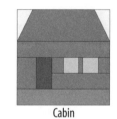

Cabin

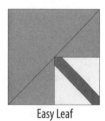

Easy Leaf

Maple Leaf

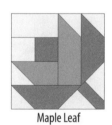

Maple Leaf

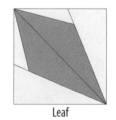

Leaf

Silver Maple

Oak Leaf

Red Oak

Sweetgum

Maple

Ivy

Complex Maple Leaf

3 Foundation Pieced
Log Cabins

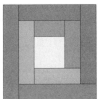

3 Log Cabin

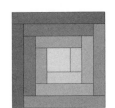

4 Log Cabin

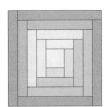

5 Log Cabin

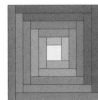

6 Log Cabin

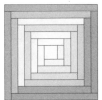

7 Log Cabin

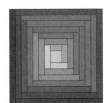

8 Log Cabin

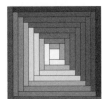

9 Log Cabin

Quarter 3 Log Cabin

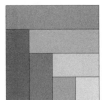

Quarter 4 Log Cabin

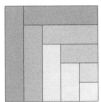

Quarter 5 Log Cabin

Quarter 6 Log Cabin

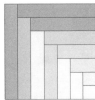

Quarter 7 Log Cabin

Quarter 8 Log Cabin

Quarter 9 Log Cabin

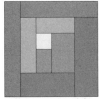

Off-Center 3 Log Cabin

Off-Center 4 Log Cabin

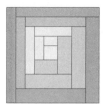

Off-Center 5 Log Cabin

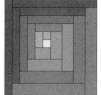

Off-Center 6 Log Cabin

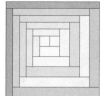

Off-Center 7 Log Cabin

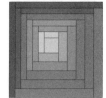

Off-Center 8 Log Cabin

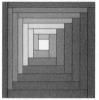

Off-Center 9 Log Cabin

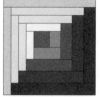

Off-Center Log Cabin

Wild Goose Log Cabin

Quarter Cabin

Diamond-in-Square
Log Cabin

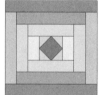

Diamond Center Log
Cabin

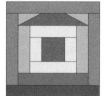

Log Cabin House

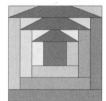

Log Cabin Pine

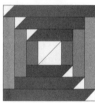

Marching Triangles

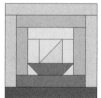

Log Cabin Boat

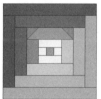

Wren House

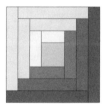

Log Cabin

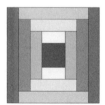

Courthouse Steps

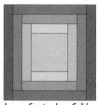

Large Center Log Cabin

Split Center Log Cabin

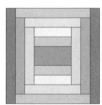

Rectangular Center Log
Cabin

Log Cabin

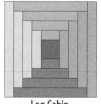

Log Cabin

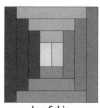

Log Cabin

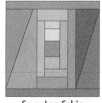

Crazy Log Cabin

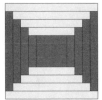

Courthouse Steps 2

3 Foundation Pieced
New York Beauties

Basic New York Beauty

Checked Arc Beauty

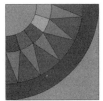

Checked Arc Beauty 2

Sunburst Beauty

Checked Arc Beauty 3

Overlapped Triangle Beauty

Starshine Beauty

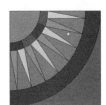

New York Compass

Shadow Arc Beauty

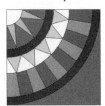

Checked Arc Beauty 4

Rick Rack Beauty

New York Nightime

Rick Rack Beauty 2

New York Sunburst

Overlapped Triangle Beauty 2

Radiant Beauty

Rolling Wheel Beauty

Four Fan Beauty

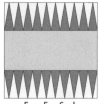

Four Fan Sash

Four Fan Beauty 2

Four Fan Sash 2

Four Fan Beauty 3

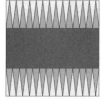

Four Fan Sash 3

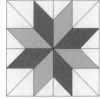

Four Fan Corner Star

3 Foundation Pieced
Pineapples

Pineapple

Pineapple 2

Pineapple 3

Pineapple 4

Pineapple 5

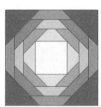

Pineapple 6

Pineapple 7

Pineapple 8

Pineapple 9

Pineapple 10

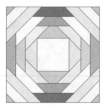

Pineapple 11

Pineapple Album

Pineapple Album 2

Pineapple Album 3

Pineapple Album 4

Pineapple Album 5

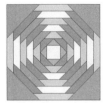

Tight Pineapple 1

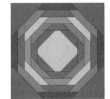

Tight Pineapple 2

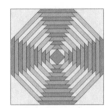

Tight Pineapple 3

Tight Pineapple 4

Tight Pineapple 5

Tight Pineapple 6

Tight Pineapple 7

3 Foundation Pieced
Stained Glass Blocks

Stained Glass Diamond
in Square

Stained Glass Diamond
in Square 2

Stained Glass Diamond
in Square 3

Stained Glass Diamond
in Square 4

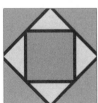

Stained Glass Diamond
in Square 5

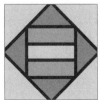

Stained Glass Diamond
with Borders

Stained Glass Cracker

Stained Glass H

Stained Glass Cracker 2

Stained Glass Diamond
in Square 6

Stained Glass Diamond
in Square 7

Stained Glass 7 Twist

Stained Glass 6 Twist

Stained Glass
Pineapple 1

Stained Glass
Pineapple 2

Stained Glass
Pineapple 3

Stained Glass
Pineapple 4

Stained Glass
Pineapple 5

Stained Glass
Pineapple 6

Stained Glass Log Cabin
Triangle

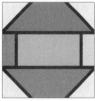

Stained Glass American
Chain

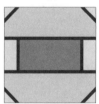

Stained Glass Circle

Stained Glass Blunt
Square on Point

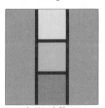

Stained Glass
Surrounded Square

Stained Glass Log Cabin
Variation

Stained Glass Log Cabin
Variation 2

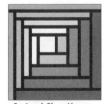

Stained Glass Log Cabin

Stained Glass Uneven
Log Cabin

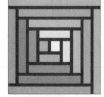

Stained Glass Log
Cabin 2

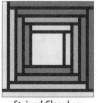

Stained Glass Log
Cabin 3

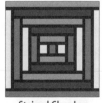

Stained Glass Log
Cabin 4

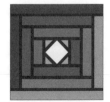

Stained Glass Log
Cabin 5

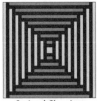

Stained Glass Log
Cabin 6

Stained Glass Stripes

Stained Glass Stripes 2

3 Foundation Pieced
Stained Glass Pictures

Stained Glass House

Stained Glass House 2

Stained Glass Heart

Stained Glass Heart 2

Stained Glass Flag

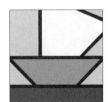

Stained Glass Sailboat

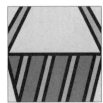

Stained Glass Basket

Stained Glass Candle

Stained Glass Flower

Stained Glass Tree 1

Stained Glass Tree 2

Stained Glass Tree 3

Stained Glass Pine
Tree 1

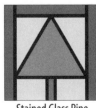

Stained Glass Pine
Tree 2

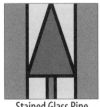

Stained Glass Pine
Tree 3

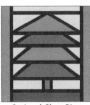

Stained Glass Pine
Tree 4

Quarter Woven Star

Quarter Woven Star 2

Quarter Crossing Points

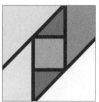

Quarter Star in a Star

Quarter T's

Quarter Star Flower

Quarter Star with Triangles

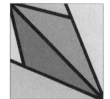

Quarter Leaf

Quarter Cross

Quarter Box-in-Box

Quarter Diagonal Triangles

Quarter Windmill

Quarter Rose

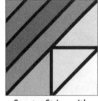

Quarter Stripe with Diamond

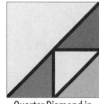

Quarter Diamond in Square

Quarter Geese Block

Quarter Geese Block 2

Quarter Rose Blooming

Quarter Emerald City

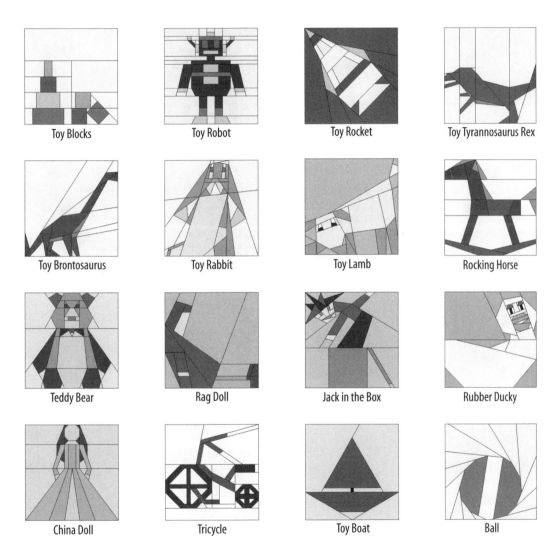

Toy Blocks	Toy Robot
Toy Rocket	Toy Tyrannosaurus Rex
Toy Brontosaurus	Toy Rabbit
Toy Lamb	Rocking Horse
Teddy Bear	Rag Doll
Jack in the Box	Rubber Ducky
China Doll	Tricycle
Toy Boat	Ball

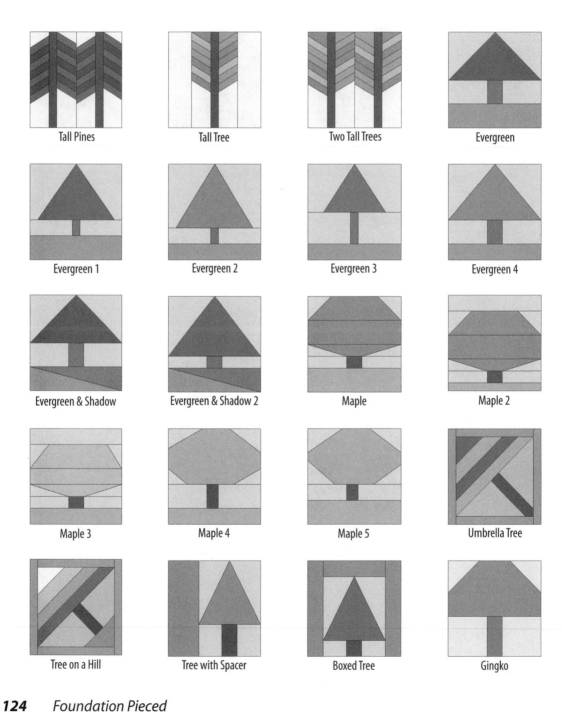

Tall Pines

Tall Tree

Two Tall Trees

Evergreen

Evergreen 1

Evergreen 2

Evergreen 3

Evergreen 4

Evergreen & Shadow

Evergreen & Shadow 2

Maple

Maple 2

Maple 3

Maple 4

Maple 5

Umbrella Tree

Tree on a Hill

Tree with Spacer

Boxed Tree

Gingko

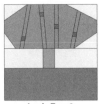
Apple Tree

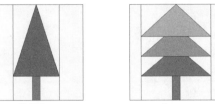
Apple Tree 2

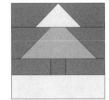
Snow-topped Tree

Christmas Tree

Tall Pine

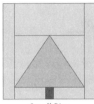
Spruce

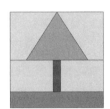
Spruce 2

Spruce 3

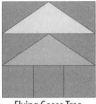
Flying Geese Tree

Small Pine

Tiny Pine

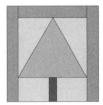
Pine

Pine 2

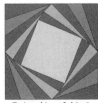
Pine 3

Pine 4

Pine 5

3 Foundation Pieced

Twists

Twisted Log Cabin 1

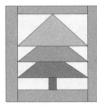
Twisted Log Cabin 2

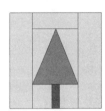
Twisted Log Cabin 3

Twisted Log Cabin 4

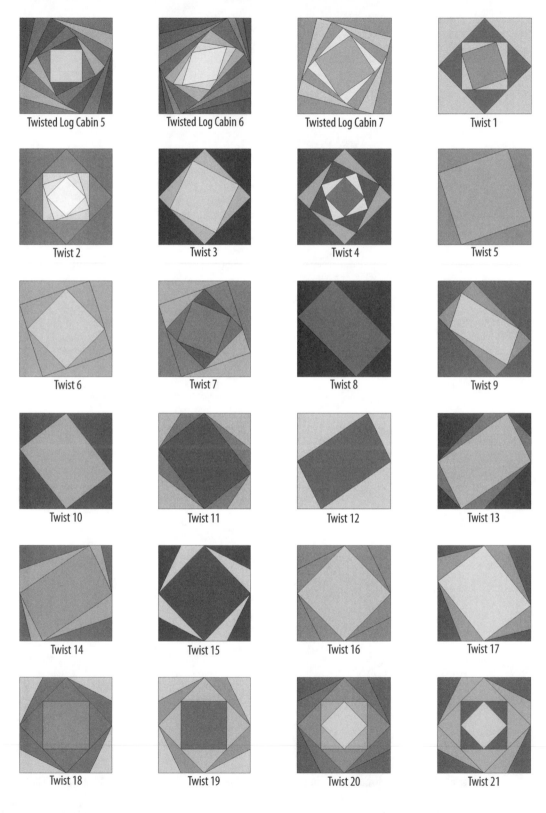

Twisted Log Cabin 5   Twisted Log Cabin 6   Twisted Log Cabin 7   Twist 1

Twist 2   Twist 3   Twist 4   Twist 5

Twist 6   Twist 7   Twist 8   Twist 9

Twist 10   Twist 11   Twist 12   Twist 13

Twist 14   Twist 15   Twist 16   Twist 17

Twist 18   Twist 19   Twist 20   Twist 21

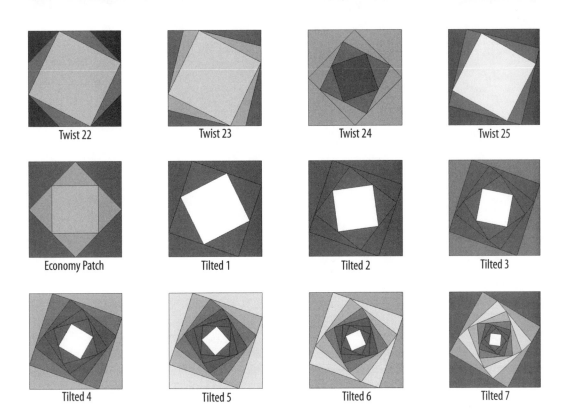

Twist 22

Twist 23

Twist 24

Twist 25

Economy Patch

Tilted 1

Tilted 2

Tilted 3

Tilted 4

Tilted 5

Tilted 6

Tilted 7

4 Classic Appliqué

Baskets 130

Birds 131

Butterflies 132

Crossing Designs 133

Eight Elements...................................... 135

Flowers 136

Flowers in Vases 137

Flowers On-Point.................................. 138

Folk Art Blocks 139

Roses 140

Silhouettes - Cameos............................ 141

Silhouettes - Other 142

Sunbonnet Sue & Sam........................... 143

Vases 144

Wreaths 145

Simple Basket

Tote Basket

Long Handled Basket

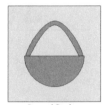

Round Basket

Basket with Handles

Picnic Basket

Frilly Basket

Basket with Ribbon

Carrying Basket

Bread Basket

Heart Basket

Flower Basket

Woven Basket

On-Point Tote Basket

On-Point Basket with Ribbon

On-Point Simple Basket

Doves

Bird in Flight

Bird with Tail Feathers

Bird Standing

Bird Sitting

Crane

Antique Woodpecker

Tropical Bird

Bird Standing 2

Bird Standing 3

Folk Art Bird

Bluebird in Flight

Bluebird by Nancy Cabot, 1944

Antique Dove

Antique Eagle

Antique Redbird

Bird from Album Quilt

Bird from Album Quilt 2

Wren

Swan

Antique Eagle 2

4 Classic Appliqué

Butterflies

Butterfly 3

Butterfly 4

Fancy Butterfly from
Grandmother Clark

Butterfly with Curling
Antennae

Butterfly with
Scalloped Wings

Butterflies in Flight

Butterfly from
Baltimore Album

Swallowtail Butterfly

Butterfly from 40s Quilt

Butterfly from 30s Quilt

Folk Art Butterfly

Butterfly 2

Butterfly from
Tennessee Quilt

Butterfly Ring

Butterfly Ring 2

Butterfly from 1936

Moth

Swallowtail Butterfly 2

Butterflies in Flight

Butterfly and Flower

4 Classic Appliqué
Crossing Designs

Clovers and Spades

Thirties Blossoms

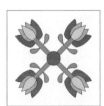

Antique Tulips

Rose with Buds

Antique Tulip Cross

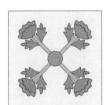

Carnation Cross

Japanese Bamboo

Tulip Tree Leaves

Tulips

Oak Leaves

Sweet Peas

Tulips 2

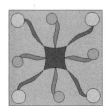

Alabama Album Quilt

Mexican Rose

Mexican Rose 2

Crossing Roses

Bottle Brush

Bud Block

Peonies

Lollipop Flowers

Circle Rose

Circle Rose 2

Comb

Oak Leaf & Reel

Oak Leaf Wreath

Oak Leaf Wreath 2

Oak Leaf Wreath 3

Crossing Branches

19th-century Leaves

Baltimore Block

Trellis Vines

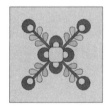
Peacock Feathers

Leaf Medallion

Spades on Spades

Iron Gate

Eight Elements

Plumes

Rose of Sharon

Tulip Cross

North Carolina Tulip Cross

Tulip and Pomegranate

Pineapple Cross

Sharon's Love

Tulip Brocade

Peony Blossoms

Mexican Rose 3

English Rose

English Rose 2

Mexican Rose

Hearts & Sunflowers

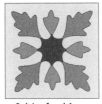

Oak Leaf and Acorn

Oak Leaf and Acorn 2

Clematis

Chrysanthemum

Tulip from North
Carolina Quilt

Tulip from North
Carolina Quilt 2

Tulip Appliqué

Poinsettia

Flower of Christmas
from Marie Webster

Single Flower

Flowers from Antique
Sampler Quilt

Flowers from Antique
Sampler Quilt 2

Poinsettia 2

Rose in Bud

Rose of Sharon from
Tennessee

Tulip from North
Carolina

Black Tulip

Hearts and Flowers

Cock's Comb and
Currants

Bleeding Heart from
Grandma Dexter

Flowers in Vases

Basket Variation

Vase with Mixed
Bouquet

Tulips from 1855
Album Quilt

Pot of Roses

Flowers in Pitcher

Tiger Lily

Tulip Bowl from North
Carolina

English Flower Pot

Ohio Tulips

Nosegay Quilt from
McKim Studios

Flowers in Heart Vase

Horn of Plenty

Kentucky Flowerpot

Rose of Sharon

Kansas Beauty

Tulips in Urn

Tulips in Pot

Bouquet from Album
Quilt

Tulip Tree 2

Flowers from Antique Sampler

Flower Pot

Kansas Beauty On-Point

Tulip Appliqué

Tulip Tree

Spring Tulips

Tulips in Urn On-Point

Rose of Sharon On-Point

Nebraska Tulips

North Carolina Tulip

Carnations in Bloom

Lily Pond from Ladies Art Company

Tulip Garden

Dutch Tulip

Tulip and Sun

First-place Flower

Rose & Buds

Three-Part Flower

Three-Part Flower 2

Stencil Tulips

Large Tulip

Posey

Pennsylvania Dutch

Folk Tulip

Mexican Rose

Rose

Day Lilies

Mexican Rose Bush

4 Classic Appliqué

Folk Art Blocks

Rooster Weathervane

Eagle with Berries

Folk Bird

Pennsylvania Dutch

Wreath Stencil

Hex Sign

Old German Design

American Star

Pineapple ca. 1850

Pineapple Design

Coxcomb in Pot

Folk Art Flower

Pennsylvania Tulip

Pomegranate

Antique Baltimore
Album House

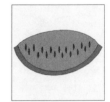

Watermelon

4 Classic Appliqué

Roses

Rose in Bloom

Rose of Sharon

Rose of LeMoyne

Rose Appliqué

Rose of Sharon

Rose Bouquet with
Stars

Rose Tree

Rose of Sharon from
McKim Studios

Old Rose of Sharon
from Canada

Radical Rose

Old Tulips

Rose from New Jersey
Sampler

Rose of Sharon

Rose of Sharon

Rosebuds

Rose Wreath 2

Rose Wreath

Rose Ring

Cabbage Rose Wreath

Rose of Sharon Wreath

Topeka Rose

4 Classic Appliqué

Silhouettes - Cameos

Mervin

Bessie

Sylvia

Katherine

Heidi

Rita

Letitia

Meredith

Sophia

Charlotte

Amanda

Georgia

Christina

Emily

Andrew

James

4 Classic Appliqué
Silhouettes - Other

Cow

Deer

Dog

Bowl of Fruit

Hen and Chicks

Horse

Man

Woman

Rooster

Kissing Birds

Birds on Bough

Eagle with Talons

Eagle

Eagle

Butterfly

Simple Bird

4 Classic Appliqué
Sunbonnet Sue & Sam

Sunbonnet Girl with
Watering Can

Sunbonnet Girl with
Bouquet

Colonial Lady

Dutch Girl

Cowboy Sue

Bonnet Baby Girl from
McKim Studios

Bonnet Baby Boy from
McKim Studios

Sunbonnet Sue

Valentine Sue

Bashful Sam

Sunbonnet Sue

Sunny Jim

Sue Picks Tulips

Overall Bill

Sue Redux

Sam

Sue with Balloons

Sue On-point

4 Classic Appliqué
Vases

Simple Vase

Simple Urn

Water Pitcher

Decorative Vase

Garden Urn

Striped Vase

Lacework Pot

Classic Urn

Large Garden Urn

Vase with Handles

Fluted Urn

Vase

Flower Pot

Ribbed Vase

Watering Can

Fan Vase

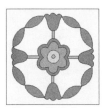

Rose and Tulip from
Grandma Dexter

Rose Wreath from New
Jersey Sampler

Floral Wreath from
Grandma Dexter

Christmas Cactus

Cherry Wreath

Daisy Wreath

Oak and Acorn Wreath

Valentine Wreath

Flower and Bud Wreath

Hearts & Ribbons

Forget-Me-Not Ring

Ribbon Medallion

Nosegay Wreath

Forget-Me-Not Wreath

Wildflower Wreath

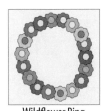

Wildflower Ring

Tulip Ring

Poinsettia Wreath

Flower Wreath

Oak and Acorn Wreath
2

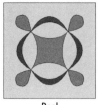

Reel

Flower Wreath 2

5 Contemporary Appliqué

Bugs 148

Cats 149

Celebrations... 150

Children 151

Christmas 152

Day in the Country................................. 154

Dogs 157

Easter 158

Fish 159

Flowers... 160

Fruit 163

Hawaiian 164

Hearts 165

Holiday 166

Music 167

Purses... 168

Shoes.. 169

Sports... 170

Teddy Bears 171

Tile and Celtic Designs 172

Toys 173

Your Design Studio 175

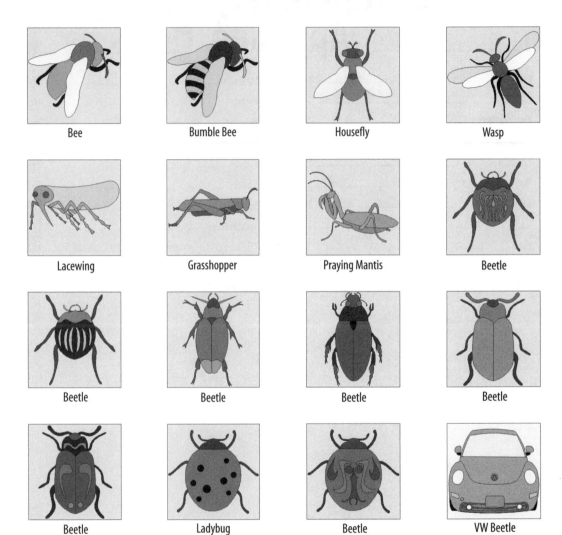

Bee	Bumble Bee	Housefly	Wasp
Lacewing	Grasshopper	Praying Mantis	Beetle
Beetle	Beetle	Beetle	Beetle
Beetle	Ladybug	Beetle	VW Beetle

Abyssinian Cat

Tabby

Kitten

Burmese Cat

Maine Coon Cat

Snowshoe Cat

Oriental Short Hair

Sleepy Cat

Cat

Calico Cartoon Cat

Smiling Cartoon Cat

Prowling Cat Silhouette

Cat with Ball Silhouette

Standing Cat Silhouette

Sitting Cat Silhouette

Hungry Cat Silhouette

Walking Cat Silhouette

Cartoon Cat Silhouette

Mates for Life (Rita Denenberg)

Our Wedding (Rita Denenberg)

Peonies and Lilacs (Rita Denenberg)

Our Vase (Rita Denenberg)

Ribbon

Dove Corner Block (Rita Denenberg)

Information Please (Rita Denenberg)

Gazebo

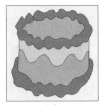

Cake

Gift Package

Gift Package

Gift Package

Baby's First Birthday

Family Tree (Rita Denenberg)

Our House (Rita Denenberg)

Stork and Baby

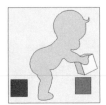

Baby with Blocks

Girl with Toy Cat

Baby Bath

Little Bo Peep and Sheep

Humpty Dumpty

Bird and Bell Toy

Boy and Butterfly

Boy and Dog

Puppy

Boy with Cake

Giraffe Toy

Giraffe Toy

Ballerina

Birthday Toys and Ribbon

Girl with Chicks

Boy with Train

Elephant Toy

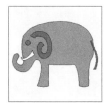

Elephant Toy

Bunny with Tulip (Rita Denenberg)

Teddy Bear with Tulip (Rita Denenberg)

Sleigh

Reindeer

Stocking

Santa

Angel with Harp

Teddy Bear and Gift

Rocking Horse

Drum

Gift

Horn

Bell

Snowman

Bells with Holly

Ornaments with Holly

Dove Ornament

Candy Canes

Holly

Ornament with Star

Ribbon

Holly Border

Ornaments

Star

Candle

Candle and Holly

Dove

Partridge

Pears

Poinsettia

Snowflake

Wreath

Nutcracker

Ring Those Bells (Rita Denenberg)

Angel with Candle

Rudolph the Red-Nosed Reindeer

Poinsettia

Ann's Angel

Candle and Holder

Christmas Tree

Tree in the Snow

Candle

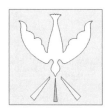

Peace Dove (Rita Denenberg)

Angel (Rita Denenberg)

Christmas Tree (Rita Denenberg)

Wise Men (Rita Denenberg)

Presents (Rita Denenberg)

Christ Child (Rita Denenberg)

Christmas Stocking (Rita Denenberg)

Fireplace at Christmas (Rita Denenberg)

Pointsettia Border (Rita Denenberg)

Noel (Rita Denenberg)

Wreath (Rita Denenberg)

Coming Home (Rita Denenberg)

Polar Bear

Polar Bear and Stars

Penguin

5 Contemporary Appliqué

Day in the Country

Christmas Goose

Christmas Goose

Goose

Goose

Duck

Duck 2

Duckling

Hen

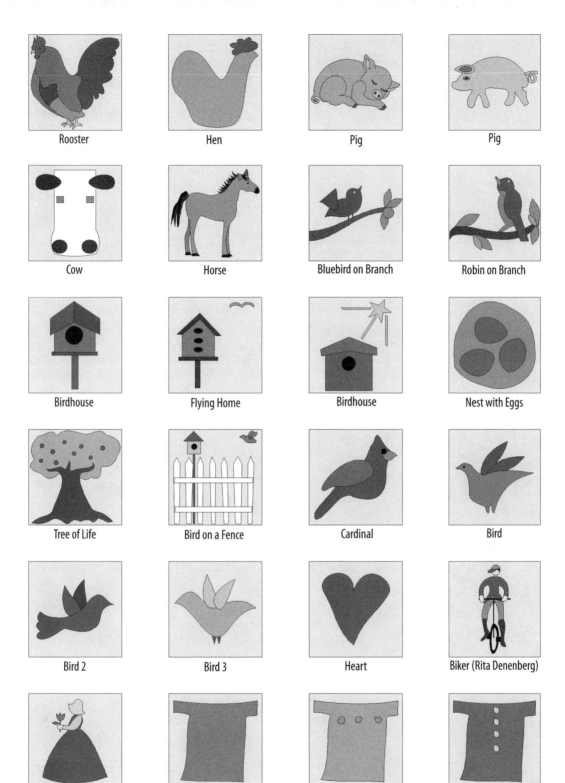

Rooster

Hen

Pig

Pig

Cow

Horse

Bluebird on Branch

Robin on Branch

Birdhouse

Flying Home

Birdhouse

Nest with Eggs

Tree of Life

Bird on a Fence

Cardinal

Bird

Bird 2

Bird 3

Heart

Biker (Rita Denenberg)

Sunbonnet (Rita Denenberg)

Dress on a Clothesline

Dotted Dress

Dress with Buttons

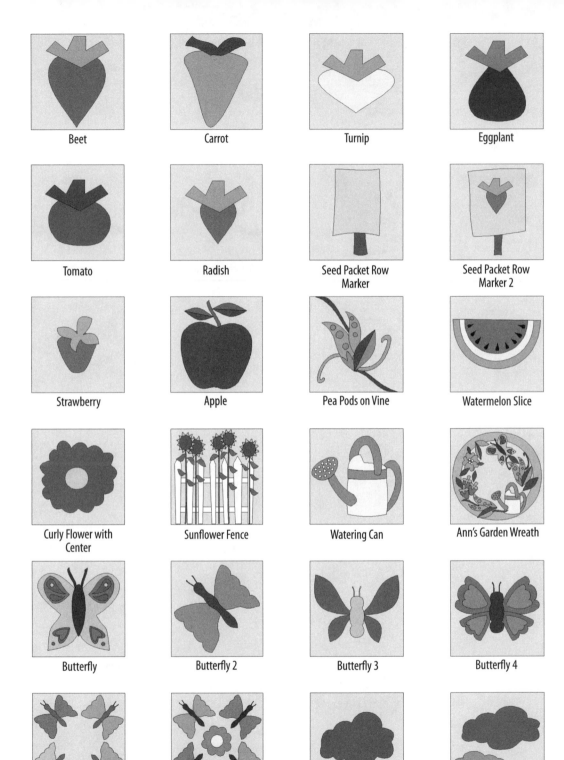

Beet

Carrot

Turnip

Eggplant

Tomato

Radish

Seed Packet Row Marker

Seed Packet Row Marker 2

Strawberry

Apple

Pea Pods on Vine

Watermelon Slice

Curly Flower with Center

Sunflower Fence

Watering Can

Ann's Garden Wreath

Butterfly

Butterfly 2

Butterfly 3

Butterfly 4

Butterflies

Butterflies and Blossom

Cloud

Two Clouds

Thundercloud

Sun

Man in the Moon

Crescent Moon

Big Dipper

Little Dipper

5 Contemporary Appliqué
Dogs

Aevi (Shiba Inu)

Sydney (German Shepard)

Baron VanBarker (Daschund)

Jock (Scottie)

Sadie (Lab)

Dog Silhouette

Lady (Cocker Spaniel)

Jumping Dog

Corgi

Surprise

Girl Walking a Dog

Boy Walking a Dog

Beans (Pug)

Welcome Home

Cartoon Dog

Happy Puppy

Cartoon Puppy

Dog with Ball

Sammy the Spastic
Wonder Dog

Dog Before Nap

5 Contemporary Appliqué
Easter

Rabbit

Rabbit

Easter Rabbit 1 (Rita
Denenberg)

Easter Rabbit 2 (Rita
Denenberg)

Easter Rabbit 3 (Rita
Denenberg)

Bunny

Sheep

Chick (Rita Denenberg)

Duckling in Shell

Squirrel

Easter Egg (Rita
Denenberg)

Easter Egg 2 (Rita
Denenberg)

Bunny with Egg (Rita Denenberg)

Easter Egg

Easter Lily (Rita Denenberg)

Easter Basket (Rita Denenberg)

5 Contemporary Appliqué
Fish

Goldie Fish

Edward Scissortail Fish

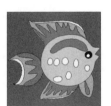
Rudy Fish

Skipper Fish

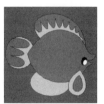
Chloe Fish

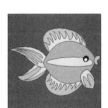
Bud Fish

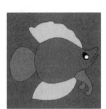
Flash Fish

Tiger Fish

Bubbles Fish

Carpie Fish

Angel Fish

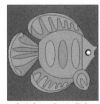
Rainbow Rosie Fish

Smoochie Fish

Jelly Bean Fish

Rocky Fish

Zoe Fish

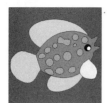

Scaley Fish

Zorro Fish

Fins Fish

Gilbert Fish

Spike Fish

Sharky Fish

Guppy Fish

Wally Fish

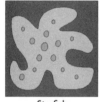

Starfish

5 Contemporary Appliqué

Flowers

Flower Sprig

Tulips

Black-Eyed Susans

Bouquet

Flowers

Tulips

Flower and Leaves

Tulip

Carnation (Rita Denenberg)

Lily (Rita Denenberg)

Pansy (Rita Denenberg)

Tiger Lily (Rita Denenberg)

Lily of the Valley (Rita Denenberg)

Gardenia (Rita Denenberg)

Sunflower (Rita Denenberg)

Rose (Rita Denenberg)

Peony (Rita Denenberg)

Lilacs (Rita Denenberg)

Daffodil (Rita Denenberg)

Bleeding Heart (Rita Denenberg)

Iris - vertical (Rita Denenberg)

Iris - on point (Rita Denenberg)

Heart of My Hearts (Rita Denenberg)

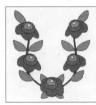

We Grew Roses (Rita Denenberg)

Rose Border (Rita Denenberg)

Two Buds

Two Buds 2

Blue Buds (quarter design)

Summer Block (quarter design)

Dahlia

Rose

Anemones (quarter design)

Contemporary Appliqué **161**

Flower in the Grass

Daisy

Peony

Three-Part Flower

Three-Part Flower 2

Rose and Buds

Rosebud

Stencil Tulips

Tulip Block

Tulip Block 2

Large Tulip

Tulip Tree

Wreath (Rita Denenberg)

Blue Buds

Summer Block

Poppies

Tyrolean Design

Shamrocks

Bouquet

Flower Pot

Flower Pot 2

Wildflower Bouquet

Sunflowers in a Pot

Painted Pot

Bird in the Buds

Garden Gate (Rita Denenberg)

Antique Birdcage (Rita Denenberg)

Roses and Butterfly

5 Contemporary Appliqué
Fruit

Apple

Apricot

Banana

Blueberries

Canteloupe

Cherries

Grapes

Grapes 2

Grapes 3

Kiwi

Lemon

Orange

Pear

Pomegranate

Raspberries

Strawberries

Hawaiian Appliqué

Tulip Hawaiian
Appliqué

Pineapple Hawaiian
Appliqué

Dolphins at Play
Hawaiian Appliqué

Palm Tree Hawaiian
Appliqué

Hawaiian Appliqué
Wreath

Hawaiian Appliqué 2

Valentine's Hawaiian
Appliqué

Hawaiian Appliqué 3

Palm Tree Hawaiian
Appliqué 2

Concentric Orchids
Hawaiian Appliqué

Hawaiian Appliqué 3

Flowering Hawaiian
Appliqué

Hawaiian Appliqué 4

Hawaiian Appliqué 5

Hawaiian Appliqué
Scroll

Stars and Hearts
Forever

Heart with Candybox
Ruffle

Heart of Leaves

Heart Ring

Garden of Hearts

Celtic Hearts with
Leaves

Celtic Hearts

Heart Flower Bouquet

Single Celtic Heart

Gumdrop Heart

Four Hearts

Four Hearts 2

Four Hearts 3

Double Hearts

Heart Blossoms

Broken Heart

Heart Flower

Heart Flower 2

Corner Hearts

Eight Hearts

Crossing Hearts

Crossing Hearts

My Hearts of Hearts
(Rita Denenberg)

Heart Dollar

Heart Scrolls

5 Contemporary Appliqué
Holiday

Shamrocks

Hat and Pipe

Cupid

Hanukkah (Rita
Denenberg)

David Star (Rita
Denenberg)

Dreidel (Rita
Denenberg)

Kikombe cha Umoja
(Unity Cup)

Bendera (Kwanzaa
Flag)

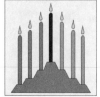
Mishumaa (7 Candles) and
Kinara (Candle Holder)

Muhindi (Corn)

Mazao (The Crops)

Trick or Treat Pumpkin

Pumpkin

Witch (Rita Denenberg)

Black Cat (Rita Denenberg)

Trick or Treat (Rita Denenberg)

Jack O'Lantern (Rita Denenberg)

Ghost (Rita Denenberg)

Bats in Web (Rita Denenberg)

New Year's Party Hat

Fireworks

Cornucopia

5 Contemporary Appliqué
Music

Sax (Rita Denenberg)

Saxophone

Saxophone with Notes

Violin (Rita Denenberg)

Big Bass (Rita Denenberg)

Guitar

Violin

Trumpet

Clarinet (Rita Denenberg)

"88" (Rita Denenberg)

Piano

Drum (Rita Denenberg)

Drum and Sticks

Musical Signs (Rita Denenberg)

Treble Clef

Treble Staff

Bass Clef

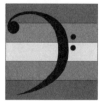

Bass Staff

Musical Note 1

Musical Note 2

Musical Note 3

The Maestro (Rita Denenberg)

5 Contemporary Appliqué

Purses

Handbag

Purse with Bow Handle

Striped Bag

Purse with Bamboo Handle

Purse Backpack

Purse with Handle

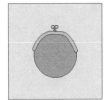

Coin Purse

Simple Tote

Purse with Flower

Striped Bag 2

Angled Purse

Buckle Closure Purse

Button up Purse

Sunflower Clutch

Striped Bag 3

Purse with Beaded Handle

5 Contemporary Appliqué

Shoes

Plain Shoe

Shoe with Bow

Shoe with Strap

Boot with Laces

Two-Tone Boot with Laces

Boot with Buttons

Shoe with Flower

Lace Shoe

Fanned Shoe

Rose Covered Shoe

Leatherwork Shoe

Lace Shoe Too

Shoe with Flower Buttons

Two-Tone Shoe

Shoe with Buckle

Strappy Shoe

5 Contemporary Appliqué
Sports

Football

Football (Rita Denenberg)

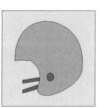
Football Helmet (Rita Denenberg)

You're #1 (Rita Denenberg)

Basketball Hoop (Rita Denenberg)

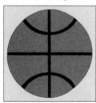
Basketball

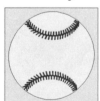
Baseball

Baseball (Rita Denenberg)

Soccer Ball

Bowling Ball (Rita Denenberg)

Bowling Pin (Rita Denenberg)

Golfball (Rita Denenberg)

The 18th Hole (Rita Denenberg)

Ice Skates (Rita Denenberg)

Roller Blade (Rita Denenberg)

Gone Fishin' (Rita Denenberg)

Boxing Gloves (Rita Denenberg)

Baseball Cap (Rita Denenberg)

Volleyball

5 Contemporary Appliqué
Teddy Bears

Teddy Bear 1

Teddy Bear 2

Teddy Bear 3

Teddy Bear 4

Teddy Bear 5

Teddy Bear 6

Teddy Bear 7

Teddy Bear with Heart

Teddy Bear with Ball

Teddy Bear with Honey

Teddy Bear with Shirt

Teddy Bear with Vest

Teddy Bear with Ice
Cream

Teddy Bear with Block

Teddy Bear with Daisy

Teddy Bear with
Daisy 2

Teddy Bear with
Daisy 3

Teddy Bear with
Flowers

5 Contemporary Appliqué

Tile and Celtic Designs

Arabesque

Moorish Tile

Fleur de Lis

Arabia

Alhambra Tile

Peacock Feathers

Byzantium

Mosaic

Islamic Tile

Grecian Tile

Roman Villa

Pompeii

Celtic Patch

Celtic Patch 2

Celtic Patch 3

Celtic Patch 4

Celtic Patch 5

Celtic Patch 6

Celtic Patch 7

Puzzle Patch

Interlocking Squares

Interlocking Squares
(border)

Ring Chain (corner)

Interlocking Rings
(border)

Interlocking Rings

5 Contemporary Appliqué
Toys

Brontosaurus

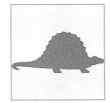

Stegosaurus

Parasauroplophus

Triceratops

Deinonychus

Tricycle

Bike

Car

Hot Air Balloon

Toy Duck

Carousel Horse (Rita Denenberg)

China Doll (Rita Denenberg)

Jack-in-the-Box

Clown Doll

Duck Pull-toy

Ted E. Bear

Train Engine Wind-up

Tractor

Car

Plane (Rita Denenberg)

Plane

Sailboat

Sailboat 2

Sailboat 3

Rocket

Toy Rocket

World Globe

Spaceman Doll

Rocket

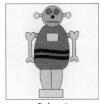

Robot 1

Robot 2

5 Contemporary Appliqué
Your Design Studio

Needle & Thread (Rita Denenberg)

Spool of Thread (Rita Denenberg)

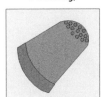

Patches (Rita Denenberg)

Scissors (Rita Denenberg)

Pincushion (Rita Denenberg)

Rotary Cutter (Rita Denenberg)

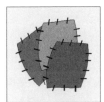

Thimble (Rita Denenberg)

Sewing Machine

Bolt of Fabric

Spool of Thread

Computer Monitor

Keyboard

Telephone

Mouse and Pad

Magnifying Glass

CD

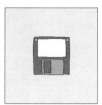

Floppy

Non-pc Computer

Computer Tower

Me (Rita Denenberg)

6 Motifs

Alphabet.. 178

Birds 181

Butterflies 182

Fish & Water Lilies 183

Flower Heads 185

Flowers with Stems 186

Folk Motifs... 187

Fruits and Veggies 188

Grapes and Vines................................... 189

Landscape Elements.............................. 190

Leaves 191

Silhouettes 193

Simple Designs 194

Sports... 195

Sunbonnet Motifs 196

Wreaths.. 197

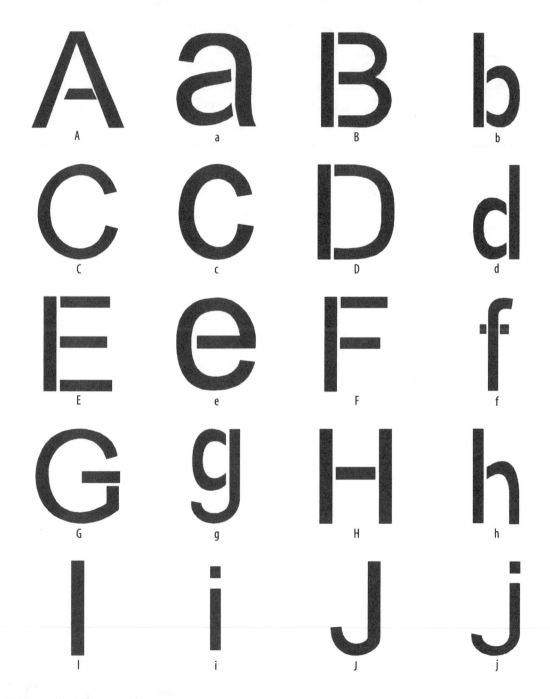

A a B b

C c D d

E e F f

G g H h

I i J j

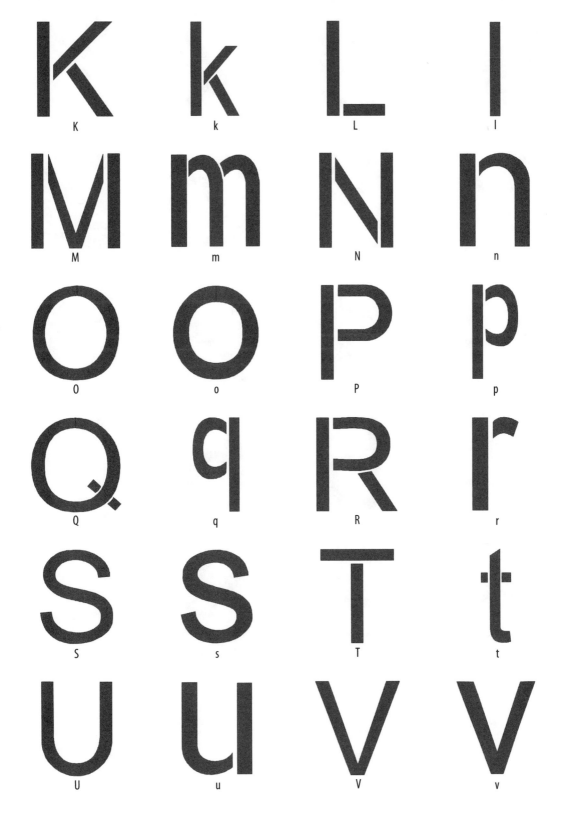

K   k   L   l

M   m   N   n

O   o   P   p

Q   q   R   r

S   s   T   t

U   u   V   v

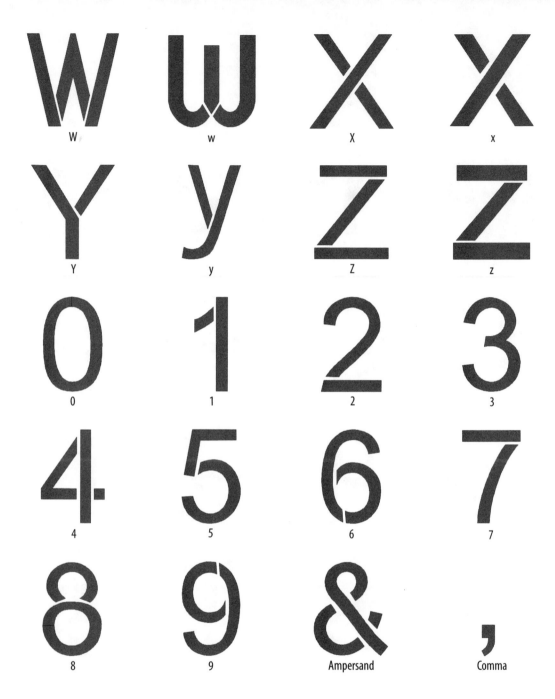

W

w

X

x

Y

y

Z

z

0

1

2

3

4

5

6

7

8

9

Ampersand

Comma

Period

Antique Bird

Antique Dove

Eagle

Folk Art Bird

Wren

Kissing Birds

Bluebird in Flight

Standing Bird 2

Standing Bird 3

Bluebird by Nancy Cabot, 1944

Chick

Bird from Album Quilt

Bird from Album Quilt 2

Bird on House

Tropical Bird

Swan

Folk Bird

Bird in Flight

Rooster

Bluebird on Branch

Robin on Branch

Dove in Flight

Cardinal

Flying Bird

Bird

Bird 2

Duck

Duck 2

Duckling

Goose

Bird in the Buds

Birdhouse

6 Motifs
Butterflies

Butterfly

Folk Art Butterfly

Butterfly from 30s Quilt

Swallowtail Butterfly

Butterfly from
Baltimore Album

Butterfly

Butterfly 2

Butterfly 3

Butterfly 4

Butterflies

Butterflies and Blossom

Butterflies 2

Butterfly with
Scalloped Wings

Swallowtail Butterfly 2

Moth

Butterfly from 1936

Butterflies in Flight

6 Motifs
Fish & Water Lilies

Goldie Fish

Edward Scissortail Fish

Rudy Fish

Skipper Fish

Chloe Fish

Bud Fish

Flash Fish

Tiger Fish

| Bubbles Fish | Carpie Fish | Angel Fish | Rainbow Rosie Fish |

| Smoochie Fish | Jelly Bean Fish | Rocky Fish | Zoe Fish |

| Scaley Fish | Zorro Fish | Fins Fish | Gilbert Fish |

| Spike Fish | Sharky Fish | Guppy Fish | Wally Fish |

| Water Lily Pad | Water Lily | Water Lily 2 | Water Lily Pads |

Water Lily Pads 2   Reeds

Sunflower	Double Tulip	Tulip and Leaves	Tulip Heads
Rose of Sharon	Zinnia	Pansy	Bud and Berries
Daffodil	Blossoms	Jonquil	Daisy
Violet Nosegay	Carnation	Orchid	Peony

North Carolina Tulip

Old Rose of Sharon
from Canada

Rose Bouquet

Single Flower

Black-Eyed Susan

Rose with Bud

Rose and Buds

Rose of LeMoyne

Rose Tree

Folk Art Flower

Flower from the 30s

Blossom and Berries

Lily

Scilla

Flower of Christmas
from Marie Webster

Rose Bud

Rose Appliqué

Pennsylvania Dutch
Flower

Daisy

Posey

Small Tulip

Pennsylvania Dutch

Rose

Circle Rose

Gloxinia

Folk Tulip

Mexican Rose

Coneflower

Coneflower 2

Black-Eyed Susan

English Rose

Sunflower in Heart

Fantasy Flower

Old-Fashioned Tulip

6 Motifs
Folk Motifs

Folk Art Leaf Motif

Pineapple Design

Folk Bird

Old German Design

Folk Art Flower

Hex Sign

Pomegranate

Folk Bird

Rooster Weathervane

Coxcomb in Pot

Pennsylvania Dutch

Pennsylvania Tulip

Eagle with Berries

Watermelon

American Star

Wreath Stencil

Eagle

6 Motifs

Fruits and Veggies

Apple

Pear

Orange

Grapes

Cherries

Strawberry

Watermelon Slice

Beet

Carrot

Turnip

Eggplant

Tomato

Radish

Pea Pod

Peas in Pods

Corn on the Cob

Relaxed Corner (In)

Relaxed Corner (Out)

Relaxed Vine

Tight Corner (In)

Tight Vine

Tight Corner (Out) with Grapes

Tight Vine with Grapes and Leaves

Tight Vine with Grapes

Grapes

Tight Grape Vine

Relaxed Corner (In)
with Leaves

Relaxed Corner (Out)
with Leaves

Relaxed Vine with
Leaves

Tight Corner (In) with
Leaves

Tight Vine with Leaves

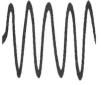

Long Vine 1

Long Vine 2

6 Motifs
Landscape Elements

Snow-covered Tree

Man in the Moon

Little Dipper

Cloud

Big Dipper

Two Clouds

Three Clouds

Star Group

Moon

Snow-covered Cabin

Smoke

Star

Moon N Stars

Moonlight 2

Twinkling Stars

Moonlight

6 Motifs
Leaves

Sweet Gum

Silver Maple

Shagbark Hickory

Stencil Leaf

White Oak

Grape Leaves

Elm

Box Elder

Palmate Leaf

Tree of Heaven

Grape Leaf

Honey Locust

Elm 2　　　　Grape Leaf 2　　　　Folk Art Leaf　　　　Folk Art Leaf 2

Antique Appliqué
Leaves　　　　Baltimore Album Leaf　　　　Holly　　　　Folk Oak

Sassafras　　　　Antique Appliqué Oak　　　　Antique Appliqué
Maple　　　　Antique Appliqué Oak

Maple Leaf　　　　Dozen-leaf Stem　　　　Dozen-leaf Stem 2　　　　Dozen-leaf Stem 3

Eleven-leaf Stem　　　　Sycamore Leaf　　　　Leaf Sprig　　　　Laurel Leaves

13-leaf Stem　　　　Oak Leaf　　　　Oak Leaf 2　　　　Oak Leaf 3

Antique Appliqué Leaf

Curled Leaf

Stencil Leaf 2

Plump Leaf

6 Motifs
Silhouettes

Cat Silhouette

Cow Silhouette

Deer Silhouette

Dog Silhouette

Fruit Bowl Silhouette

Hen with Chicks
Silhouette

Horse Silhouette

Man Silhouette

Woman Silhouette

Rooster Silhouette

Kissing Birds Silhouette

Birds on Branch
Silhouette

Eagle Silhouette

Eagle Silhouette 2

Sitting Cat Silhouette

Hungry Cat Silhouette

Dog Silhouette 2

Jumping Dog
Silhouette

6 Motifs
Simple Designs

Sun

Heart

Star

Moon

Ice Cream Cone

Tent

Balloons

Rainbow

Flower

Cow

Moorish Design

Happy Face

House

Tree

Apple Tree

Leaf

Football

Football Helmet

Basketball

Basketball Hoop (Rita Denenberg)

Baseball

Baseball Cap (Rita Denenberg)

Volleyball

Ice Skate (Rita Denenberg)

Roller Skate (Rita Denenberg)

Bowling Ball (Rita Denenberg)

Bowling Pin (Rita Denenberg)

You're #1 (Rita Denenberg)

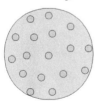

Golf Ball (Rita Denenberg)

The 18th Hole (Rita Denenberg)

Ball

Boxing Gloves (Rita Denenberg)

Gone Fishin' (Rita Denenberg)

Sunbonnet Motifs

Sunbonnet Sue

Sitting Sue

Sue with Pocket

Sue Redux

Sun Bonnet Girl from
Grandmother Clark, 1931

Sun Bonnet Girl with
Bouquet

Colonial Girl

Sunbonnet Sue as Little
Bo Peep

Sunbonnet Sue as Little
Boy Blue

Valentine Sue

Sue Picks Tulips

Sue with Balloons

Sam

Bashful Sam

Sunny Jim

Overall Bill

Cosmos Wreath

Wind Blown Rose

Scattered Roses

Tulips in a Tangle

Rose and Buds
Quatrefoil

Daisy Cluster

Rose Sprigs

Tulip Ring

Zinnia Ring

Scattered Blossoms

Buds in a Circle

Grape Leaf Wreath

Stencil Leaf Wreath

Oak Leaf Wreath

Antique Leaf Wreath

Hickory Wreath

Curled Leaf Wreath

7 Quilting Stencils

Border Stencils 200

Boxes 201

Celtic Interweaves 202

Curves 203

Feathers 204

Flowers 205

Hearts 206

Leaves 207

Ribbons 208

Stars and Snowflakes 209

Straight and Curved Lines 210

Wreaths 211

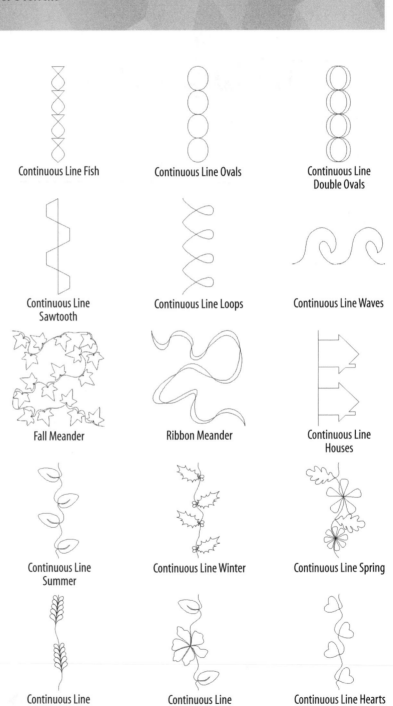

Continuous Line Stars

Continuous Line Fish

Continuous Line Ovals

Continuous Line Double Ovals

Continuous Line Diamonds

Continuous Line Sawtooth

Continuous Line Loops

Continuous Line Waves

Continuous Greek Key

Fall Meander

Ribbon Meander

Continuous Line Houses

Feather Meander

Continuous Line Summer

Continuous Line Winter

Continuous Line Spring

Continuous Line Fall

Continuous Line Feathers

Continuous Line Flowers

Continuous Line Hearts

Heart & Ribbon
Meander

Leaf Meander

Continuous Line Moon
& Stars

Continuous Line Bells

Continuous Line Maple
Leaves

7 Quilting Stencils
Boxes

Boxed Diagonals 1

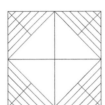

Boxed Diagonals 2

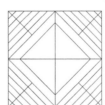

Boxed Diagonals 3

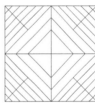

Boxed Diagonals 4

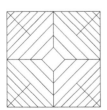

Boxed Diagonals 5

Crossing Squares

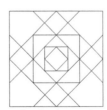

Crossing Squares 2

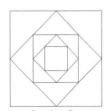

Box-in-a-Box

Box-in-a-Box 2

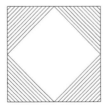

Box-in-a-Box 3

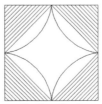

Box-in-a-Box 4

Box-in-a-Box 5

Box-in-a-Box 6

Box-in-a-Box 7

Diamonds

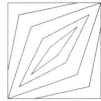

Diamonds 2

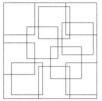

Overlapping Boxes 1

Overlapping Boxes 2

Overlapping Boxes 3

7 Quilting Stencils
Celtic Interweaves

Celtic Circle

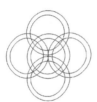

Interlocking Rings

Rings and Squares

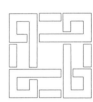

Celtic Interweave

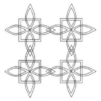

Celtic Squares and Loops

Celtic Rope

Rings and Squares 2

Celtic Squares and Loops 2

Interwoven Square

Looped Rings

Interlocking Squares

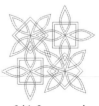

Celtic Squares and Loops 3

Ring Chain (corner)

Interlocking Rings
(border)

Interlocking Rings

Interlocking Squares
(border)

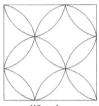

Wineglass

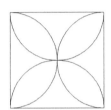

Wineglass 2

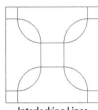

Interlocking Lines

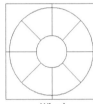

Wheel

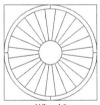

Wheel 2

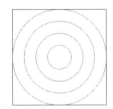

Circle-in-a-Circle

Circle-in-a-Circle 2

Off-side Circles

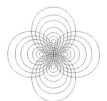

Peacock Feather Stencil

Four Off-Side Circles

Bullseye

Pumpkin Seeds

Pumpkin Seeds 2

Pumpkin Seeds 3

Clover

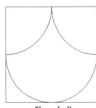

Clamshell

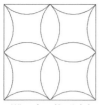

Wineglass (Straight)

Seeds & Waves

7 Quilting Stencils
Feathers

Feather (vertical)

Feather

Feather Plume with Ovals

Feathers with Heart

Feathers 4

Feathers 5

Feathers 6

Twisting Feathers

Twisting Feathers 2

Feather Ring

Crossing Feathers

Feathers with Heart Mirrored

Feather (corner)

Feather (border)

Double Plume

Double-Plume Medallion

Feather Wreath 1

Feather Wreath 2

Feather Wreath 3

Feather Wreath 4

Feather Wreath 5

7 Quilting Stencils
Flowers

Flower Wreath

Rose Wreath

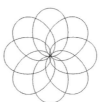

Radiating Petals

Tulip Ring

Daffodil

Rose Stencil

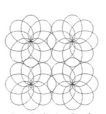

Four Radiating Petals

Blossoms Stencil

Swirling Petals

Floral Corner

Posey Wreath

Petals Stencil

Blossoms

Ring Around the Posey

Sprouting Orchids

Daisy Chain

7 Quilting Stencils
Hearts

Plain Heart

Staggered Hearts

Dozen Hearts

Nine Hearts

Double-Heart Ring

Heart Ring

Heart Ring 2

Heart Stars

Six Heart Ring

Six Heart Ring 2

Heart Tulip Ring

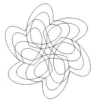

Rolling Hearts

Rolling Hearts 2

Rolling Hearts 3

Rolling Hearts 4

Rose Window

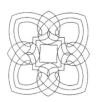

Double-Crossed Hearts

Ring of Hearts

Ribbons and Hearts

Heart Ring

Ribbons and Hearts 2

Oak Leaf and Hearts
Reel

7 Quilting Stencils
Leaves

Maple Leaves

Maple Leaf Ring

Leaves

Leaf Wreath with 4
Points

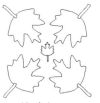

Small Leaf Wreath with
4 Points

Leaf Wreath with 5
Points

Leaf Wreath with 6
Points

Leaf Wreath

Leaves and Hearts

Oak Leaf and Reel

Oak Leaves and Berries

Leaves

Leaves 2

Leaf Cable

Leaf Ring

Leaf Ring 2

Leaf Square

Oak Leaves and Circles

Oak Leaves and Reel

Oak Leaves and Nuts

7 Quilting Stencils
Ribbons

Crossing Ribbons

Wavy Ribbon

Simple Ribbon

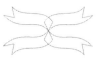

Four Ribbons

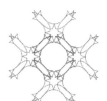

Ribbons and Stars

Simple Ribbon 2

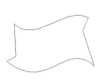

Banner

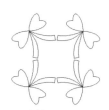

Ribbon Frame

Simple Ribbon 3

Fat Ribbon

Ribbon with Three Bows

Ribbon Frame 2

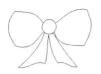

Fat Ribbon 2

Ribbon Wreath

Ribbon Vine

Ribbon Wreath 2

7 Quilting Stencils
Stars and Snowflakes

Star Swirl

Crystal Snowflake

Christmas Snowflake

Cutout Snowflake

Arabesque

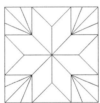

Stars & Beams

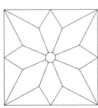

Star

Star Wreath

Star 2

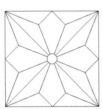

Star-in-Square

Starburst

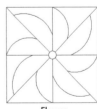

Flower

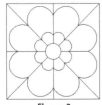

Flower 2

Flower 3

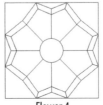

Flower 4

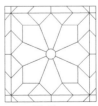

Tile Floor

Stars

Tile Overall

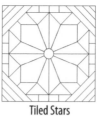

Tiled Stars

7 Quilting Stencils
Straight and Curved Lines

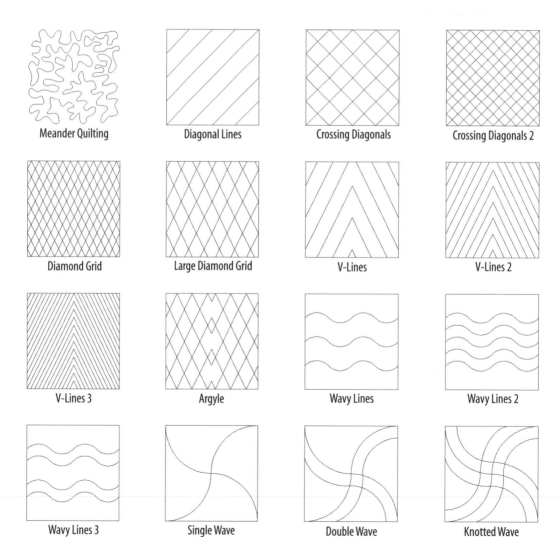

Meander Quilting   **Diagonal Lines**   **Crossing Diagonals**   **Crossing Diagonals 2**

Diamond Grid   **Large Diamond Grid**   **V-Lines**   **V-Lines 2**

V-Lines 3   **Argyle**   **Wavy Lines**   **Wavy Lines 2**

Wavy Lines 3   **Single Wave**   **Double Wave**   **Knotted Wave**

Waving Grid	Scallops	Double Scallop	Wavy & Straight
Thirteen Lines	Seven Lines	Twenty-One Lines	Eleven Lines

Six Lines

7 Quilting Stencils
Wreaths

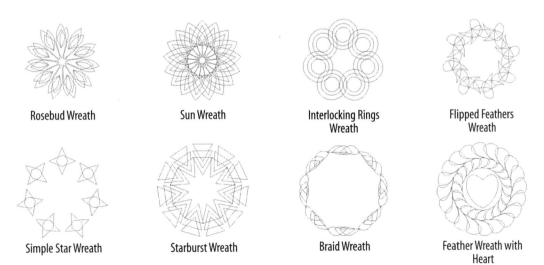

Rosebud Wreath	Sun Wreath	Interlocking Rings Wreath	Flipped Feathers Wreath
Simple Star Wreath	Starburst Wreath	Braid Wreath	Feather Wreath with Heart

Heart Wreath

Heart Wreath 2

Heart Wreath 3

Heart Wreath 4

Heart Wreath 5

Heart Wreath 6

Diamond Wreath

Sunflower Wreath

Sawtooth Wreath

Looped Ring Wreath

Circle Wreath

Petal Wreath

Petal Wreath 2

Feather Wreath

Feather Wreath 2

Feather Wreath 3

Feather Wreath 4

Simple Wreath

8 Overlaid Blocks

Embellished Alphabet 214

Fancy Flowers 215

Pictures 216

Simple Designs 218

A is for Apple

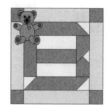

B is for Bear

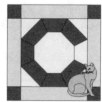

C is for Cat

D is for Dog

E is for Egg

F is for Fish

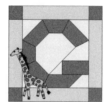

G is for Giraffe

H is for Heart

I is for Ice Cream

J is for Jack-o'-Lantern

K is for Kite

L is for Leaf

M is for Moon

N is for Needle

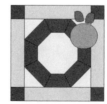

O is for Orange

P is for Penguin

Q is for Queen

R is for Robot

S is for Snowflake

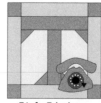

T is for Telephone

U is for Umbrella

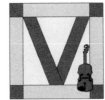
V is for Violin

W is for Watering Can

X is for Xylophone

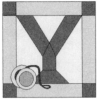
Y is for Yo Yo

Z is for Zebra

8 Overlaid Blocks
Fancy Flowers

Rose Wreath in a Diamond

Framed Christmas Wreath

Spring Flowers

Flower Sprig Star

Shady Window

Flower-in-the-Box

Bluebell Star

Striped Floral

Andrea's Fancy

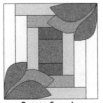
Rotate Surprise

Stained-Glass Window

Flowering Wheel

Rising Waves

Glass Sunflower

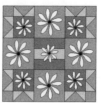

9-Patch Flower

Orange Blossom

Overlapping Hearts

Valentine Album

Whirling Buds &
Berries

Petal Snowflake

Variable Violet Star

Violet Star Bouquet

Trellis

Blooming Orchid

Scattered Leaves

Flowering Ohio Star

Fall Dance

Purple Petals

8 Overlaid Blocks
Pictures

Fish Tank

May Basket

Mother's Day Basket

Laurel & Lyre

Key West

Sailor's Delight

Fancy Fruit

Fall Flowers

Sunny Sail

First Bloom

Christmas Morning

Presents Under the Tree

Evening Sail

Snowy Day

Barn Friends

On the Lookout

Sweet Dreams

Wake Up

A Flock

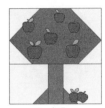

Apple Tree

Sleep Tight

8 Overlaid Blocks
Simple Designs

Fan and Stars

Stars and Stripes

Star within Stars

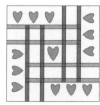

Heart Lattice

Patriotic Patch

Constellation Patch

Butterfly Star

Fantasia

Autumn Cross Patch

Framed Appliqué

Captured Feathers

Framed Stars

Diamond Flower

Spiral Roses

Fanned Flowers

Flying Stars

Rotating Stars

Now Showing

Spinning Snowflake

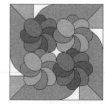

Woven Petals

Texas Wheel

Grapes of Wrath

9 Border Blocks

Checked Borders 222

Curved Borders 223

Interwoven 224

Miscellaneous 225

Picket 226

Scrolls 228

Single Block Patterns.. 229

Striped 232

Swags.. 234

Triangular 235

Vines 239

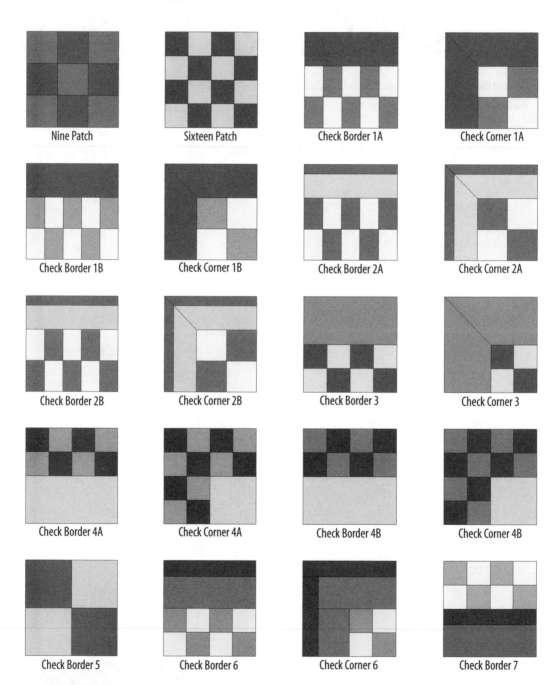

Nine Patch

Sixteen Patch

Check Border 1A

Check Corner 1A

Check Border 1B

Check Corner 1B

Check Border 2A

Check Corner 2A

Check Border 2B

Check Corner 2B

Check Border 3

Check Corner 3

Check Border 4A

Check Corner 4A

Check Border 4B

Check Corner 4B

Check Border 5

Check Border 6

Check Corner 6

Check Border 7

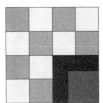

Check Corner 7

Check Border 8A

Check Corner 8A

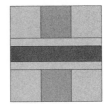

Check Border 8B

Check Corner 8B

Check Border 9

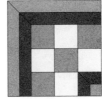

Check Corner 9

9 Border Blocks
Curved Borders

Orange Peel Border

Orange Peel Corner

Wedding Ring Border

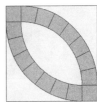

Wedding Ring Corner

Pickle Dish Border

Pickle Dish Corner

Football Border

Football Corner

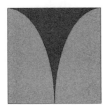

Drunkard's Path Border

Drunkard's Path Corner

Rainbow Border

Rainbow Corner

Fan Dance Border

Fan Dance Corner

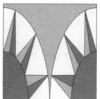

Split Sunflower Border

Split Sunflower Corner

Drunkard's Path
Border 2

Drunkard's Path
Corner 2

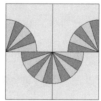

Fan Border

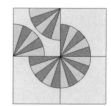

Fan Corner

Curved Path Border

Curved Path Corner

Orange Peel

Sugar Bowl

Half Sun

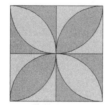

Flower Petals

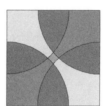

Flowering Snowball

9 Border Blocks
Interwoven

Intertwined Border

Intertwined Corner

French Knot Border

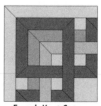

French Knot Corner

Greek Key Border

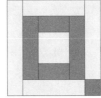

Greek Key Corner

Criss Cross Border

Criss Cross Corner

Oriental Knot Border

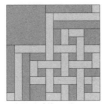

Oriental Knot Corner

Overlapped Snowflake Border

Overlapped Snowflake Corner

Double Y Border

Double Y Corner

Twisted Rope Border

Twisted Rope Corner

9 Border Blocks

Miscellaneous

Strippy Block

Hex Sign

Staccato Border

Staccato Corner

Gothic Window Border

Gothic Window Corner

Strips and Strings Border

Strips and Strings Corner

Grooves Border

Grooves Corner

Striped Grooves Border

Striped Grooves Corner

Spring Flowers Border

Spring Flowers Corner

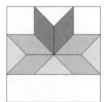

Peony Border

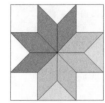

Peony Corner

Handkerchief Edge
Border

Handkerchief Edge
Corner

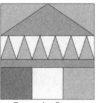

Tramp Art Frame
Border

Tramp Art Frame
Corner

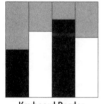

Keyboard Border

Bamboo Fence Border

9 Border Blocks
Picket

Picket Border 1

Picket Corner 1

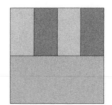

Picket Border 2

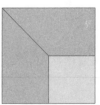

Picket Corner 2

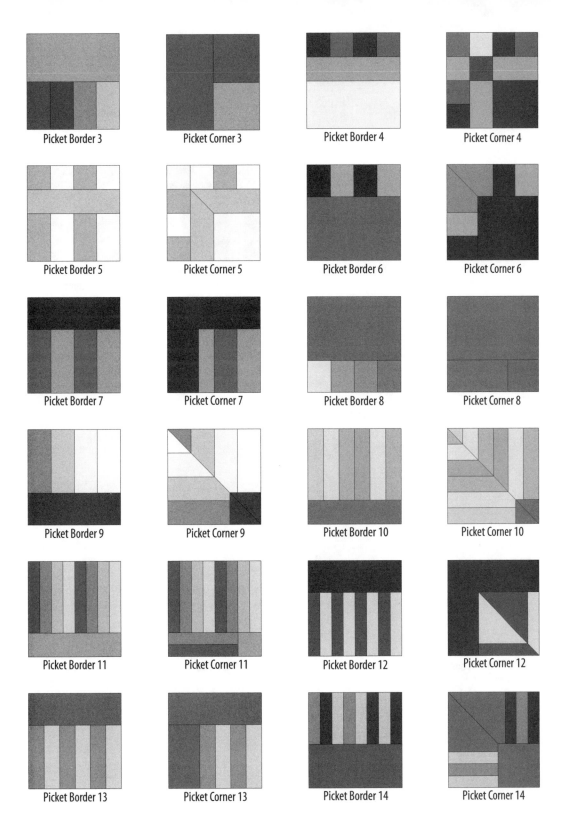

Picket Border 3

Picket Corner 3

Picket Border 4

Picket Corner 4

Picket Border 5

Picket Corner 5

Picket Border 6

Picket Corner 6

Picket Border 7

Picket Corner 7

Picket Border 8

Picket Corner 8

Picket Border 9

Picket Corner 9

Picket Border 10

Picket Corner 10

Picket Border 11

Picket Corner 11

Picket Border 12

Picket Corner 12

Picket Border 13

Picket Corner 13

Picket Border 14

Picket Corner 14

Picket Border 15

Picket Corner 15

Picket Border 16

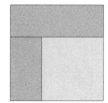

Picket Corner 16

Picket Border 17

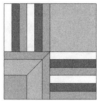

Picket Corner 17

Pickets and Points
Border

Pickets and Points
Corner

Pickets and Stripes
Border

Pickets and Stripes
Corner

9 Border Blocks

Scrolls

Scroll with Thorns and
Diamonds

Fleur de Lis

Peacocks

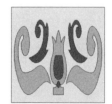

Lyre Scroll

Leaf Scroll

Grain Scroll

Berry Scroll

Folk Art Twigs and
Heart

Tulips Scrolls

Mexican Rose Scroll

Antique Flower Scroll

Comb and Currants Scroll

Brocade Scrollwork

Antique Flower Scroll 2

Bluebird Scroll

Scroll with Thorns and Diamonds 2

9 Border Blocks
Single Block Patterns

1 Diamond

1 Drop Diamond

1 Double Diamond

1 Drop Double Diamond

1 Big and Little Diamond

1 Drop Big and Little Diamond

1 Point Out

1 Point In

1 Big and Little Point Out

1 Big and Little Point In

2 Diamonds

2 Drop Diamonds

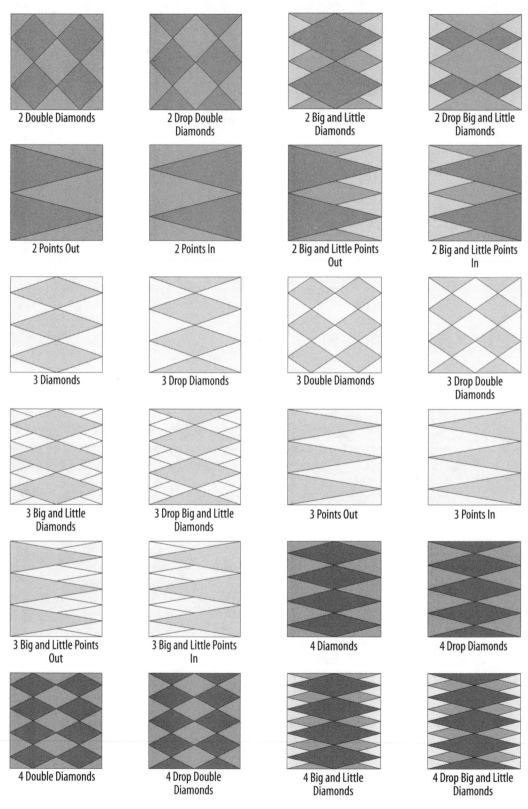

2 Double Diamonds

2 Drop Double Diamonds

2 Big and Little Diamonds

2 Drop Big and Little Diamonds

2 Points Out

2 Points In

2 Big and Little Points Out

2 Big and Little Points In

3 Diamonds

3 Drop Diamonds

3 Double Diamonds

3 Drop Double Diamonds

3 Big and Little Diamonds

3 Drop Big and Little Diamonds

3 Points Out

3 Points In

3 Big and Little Points Out

3 Big and Little Points In

4 Diamonds

4 Drop Diamonds

4 Double Diamonds

4 Drop Double Diamonds

4 Big and Little Diamonds

4 Drop Big and Little Diamonds

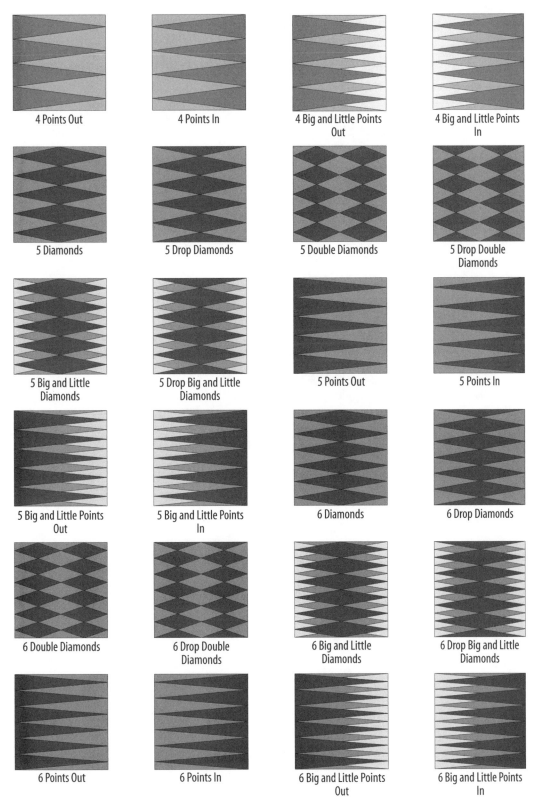

4 Points Out

4 Points In

4 Big and Little Points Out

4 Big and Little Points In

5 Diamonds

5 Drop Diamonds

5 Double Diamonds

5 Drop Double Diamonds

5 Big and Little Diamonds

5 Drop Big and Little Diamonds

5 Points Out

5 Points In

5 Big and Little Points Out

5 Big and Little Points In

6 Diamonds

6 Drop Diamonds

6 Double Diamonds

6 Drop Double Diamonds

6 Big and Little Diamonds

6 Drop Big and Little Diamonds

6 Points Out

6 Points In

6 Big and Little Points Out

6 Big and Little Points In

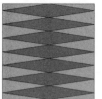

7 Diamonds

7 Drop Diamonds

7 Double Diamonds

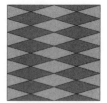

7 Drop Double
Diamonds

7 Big and Little
Diamonds

7 Drop Big and Little
Diamonds

7 Points Out

7 Points In

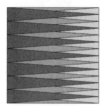

7 Big and Little Points
Out

7 Big and Little Points
In

9 Border Blocks
Striped

Stripe Border 1

Stripe Corner 1

Stripe Border 2

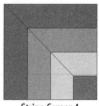

Stripe Corner 2

Stripe Border 3

Stripe Corner 3

Stripe Border 4

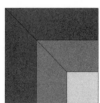

Stripe Corner 4

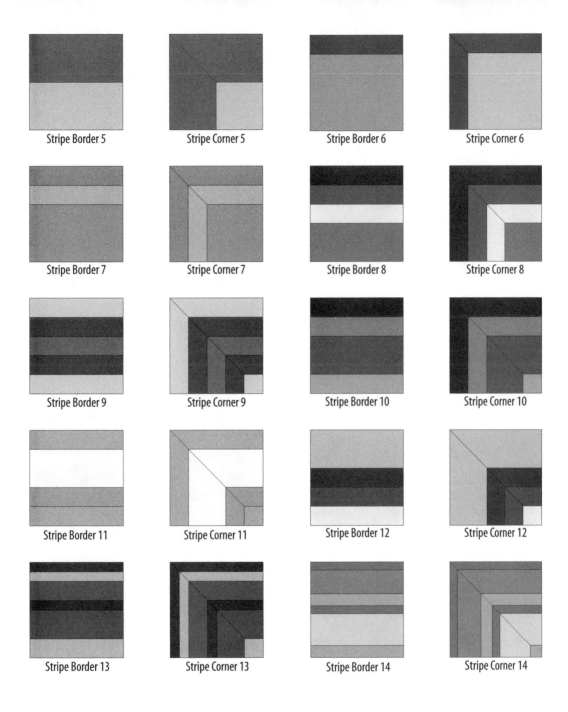

Stripe Border 5

Stripe Corner 5

Stripe Border 6

Stripe Corner 6

Stripe Border 7

Stripe Corner 7

Stripe Border 8

Stripe Corner 8

Stripe Border 9

Stripe Corner 9

Stripe Border 10

Stripe Corner 10

Stripe Border 11

Stripe Corner 11

Stripe Border 12

Stripe Corner 12

Stripe Border 13

Stripe Corner 13

Stripe Border 14

Stripe Corner 14

Plain Swag Corner

Plain Swag Border

Single Leaf Swag Border

Small Ribbon Swag Border

Double Tassle Swag Border

Scalloped Swag Border

Scalloped Swag with Small Ribbons

Scalloped Swag with Large Ribbons

Daisy Swag Border

Wildflower Swag Border

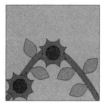

Spikey Flower Swag Border

Nosegay Swag Border

Forget-Me-Not Swag Border

Combed Swag Border

Valentine Swag Border

Double Scalloped Swag Border

9 Border Blocks
Triangular

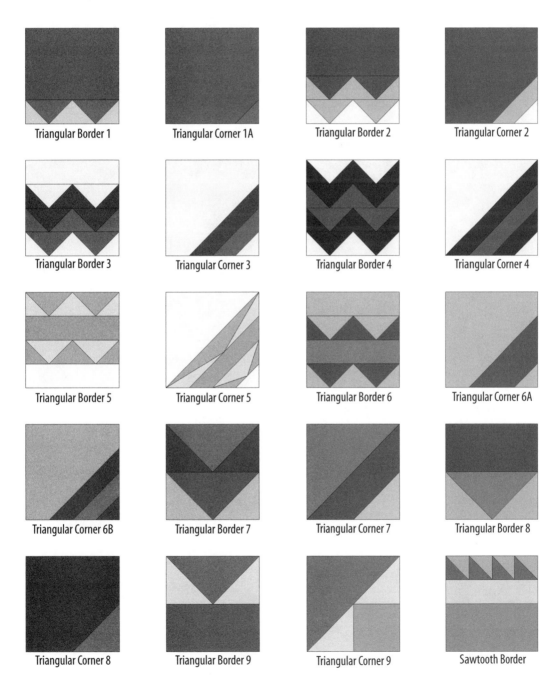

Triangular Border 1

Triangular Corner 1A

Triangular Border 2

Triangular Corner 2

Triangular Border 3

Triangular Corner 3

Triangular Border 4

Triangular Corner 4

Triangular Border 5

Triangular Corner 5

Triangular Border 6

Triangular Corner 6A

Triangular Corner 6B

Triangular Border 7

Triangular Corner 7

Triangular Border 8

Triangular Corner 8

Triangular Border 9

Triangular Corner 9

Sawtooth Border

Sawtooth Corner

Double Sawtooth
Border

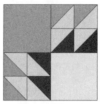

Double Sawtooth
Corner

Wild Goose Chase
Border

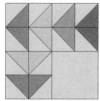

Wild Goose Chase
Corner

Diamond Border

Diamond Corner

Diamond Border 2

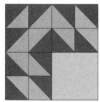

Diamond Corner 2

Check and Triangle
Border

Check and Triangle
Corner

Check and Triangle
Border 2

Check and Triangle
Corner 2

Check and Triangle
Border 3

Check and Triangle
Corner 3

Check and Triangle
Border 4

Check and Triangle
Corner 4

Stripe and Strips
Border

Stripe and Strips Corner

Stripe and Strips
Border 2

Stripe and Strips
Corner 2

Stripe and Strips
Border 3

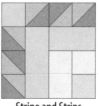

Stripe and Strips
Corner 3

Triangles and Strips
Border

Triangles and Strips
Corner

Triangles and Strips
Border 2

Triangles and Strips
Corner 2

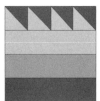

Triangles and Strips
Border 3

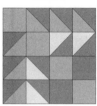

Triangles and Strips
Corner 3

Diamonds and Strips
Border

Diamonds and Strips
Corner

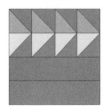

Geese and Strips
Border

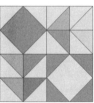

Geese and Strips Corner

Meeting Geese & Strips
Border

Meeting Geese & Strips
Corner

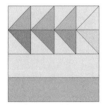

Geese and Strips
Border 2

Geese and Strips
Corner 2

Chevrons & Strips
Border

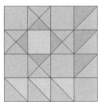

Chevrons & Strips
Corner

Slanting Stripes &
Strips Border

Slanting Stripes &
Strips Corner

Triple Slanting Strips
Border

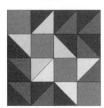

Triple Slanting Strips
Corner

Zig Zags Border

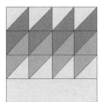

Zig Zags Corner

Triple Triangles Border

Triple Triangles Corner

Double Diamonds
Border

Double Diamonds
Corner

Meeting Double
Diamonds Border

Meeting Double
Diamonds Corner

Triangles Border

Triangles Corner

Meeting Triangles
Border

Meeting Triangles
Corner

Diamond in Square
Strips Border

Diamond in Square
Strips Corner

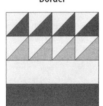

Chevrons and Stripes
Border

Chevrons and Stripes
Corner

Meeting Chevrons
Border

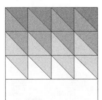

Meeting Chevrons
Corner

More Diamonds &
Strips Border

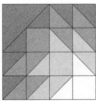

More Diamonds &
Strips Corner

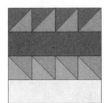

Double Diamonds
Border 2

Double Diamonds
Corner 2

Diamonds & Triangles
Border

Diamonds & Triangles
Corner

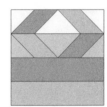

Up and Down Triangles
Border

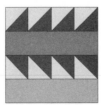

Up and Down Triangles
Corner

Tree Everlasting Border

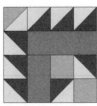

Tree Everlasting Corner

Zig Zag Border 2

Zig Zag Corner 2

Zig Zag Border 3

Zig Zag Corner 3

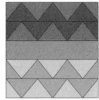

Zig Zag Border 4

Zig Zag Corner 4

Zig Zag Border 5

Zig Zag Corner 5

Delectable Mountains Border

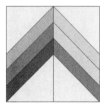

Delectable Mountains Corner

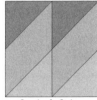

Seminole Stripes Border

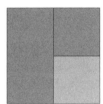

Four Patch Corner

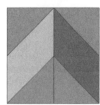

3-D Zig Zag Border

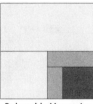

Triple 3-D Zig Zag Border

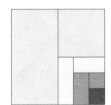

Triple 3-D Zig Zag Corner

Pinwheel Border

Y Block Border

9 Border Blocks
Vines

Relaxed Vine Corner (Out)

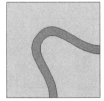

Relaxed Vine Corner (In)

Relaxed Vine

Tight Vine Corner (Out)

Tight Vine Corner (In)

Tight Vine

Relaxed Vine Corner (Out) with Leaves

Relaxed Vine Corner (In) with Leaves

Relaxed Vine with Leaves

Tight Vine Corner (Out) with Leaves

Tight Vine Corner (In) with Leaves

Tight Vine with Leaves

Tight Corner (In) with Complex Leaves

Tight Vine with Complex Leaves

Tight Corner (In) with Flower and Bud

Tight Vine with Flower and Bud

Relaxed Corner (In) with Pomegranates

Relaxed Vine with Pomegranates

Tight Corner (In) with Circle Flower

Tight Vine with Circle Flower

Relaxed Corner (In) with Flowers

Relaxed Vine with Flowers

Tight Corner (Out) with Grapes

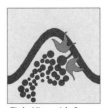

Tight Vine with Grapes

Tight Vine with Grapes and Leaves

Grapes

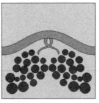

Relaxed Vine with Grapes

Relaxed Vine with Grapes and Leaves

Relaxed Grape Vine

Tight Grape Vine

Double Grapes

Grapes On-point

Relaxed Vine Corner
(Out)

Relaxed Vine with
Honeysuckle

Relaxed Corner (Out)
with Bird and Berries

Relaxed Vine with Bird
and Berries

10 Reference Information

About the Block Library 244

Searching for Blocks by Notecard 245

Searching for Blocks by Category 246

Block Categories 247

Index 249

Electric Quilt 6

About the Block Library

1 Click **LIBRARIES > Block Library.** The library opens with blocks displayed. Notice the name *Library* on the top-left.

Seeing More Categories and Styles

2 Blocks are organized into categories. Beside the list of names **drag the vertical scrollbar down to see the different categories**. In the Block Library the categories are: 1 Classic Pieced, 2 Contemporary Pieced, etc.

3 Each category has styles. **Click the plus sign next to any category name to see its styles.** For example, if you are in 4 Classic Applique (in the Block Library) you would see the styles: Birds, Butterflies, Crossing Designs, etc.

4 **Click any name to see blocks in that style.**

Seeing More Blocks in a Style

5 The number of blocks in each style is shown at the lower-right beside the horizontal scrollbar. If the style contains 57 blocks, but you only see 9, you need to scroll. **Drag the horizontal scrollbar beneath the blocks to the right to see more blocks within that style.**

6 You can also change the number of blocks that display at one time. Below the name list you will see a series of display buttons with squares on them. **Click a button with fewer squares to see fewer blocks, or one with more squares to see more blocks.** This is also a nice feature when viewing complex blocks. You can click a button with fewer squares to "zoom in" closer to see a block's detail.

Step 1

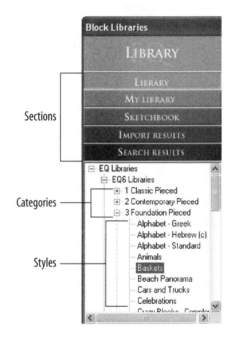

Sections

Categories

Styles

The selected category and style appear here

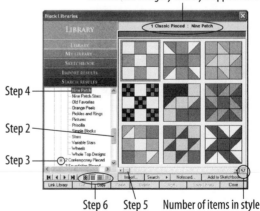

Step 4

Step 2

Step 3

Step 6   Step 5   Number of items in style

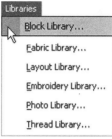

Step 1

Step 2

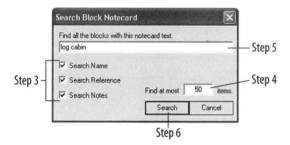

Step 5

Step 3

Step 4

Step 6

Step 6

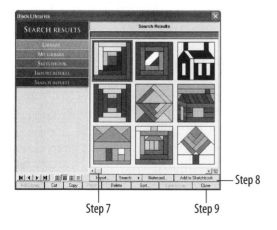

Step 8

Step 7   Step 9

Searching for Blocks by Notecard

1   Open the block library.
    (**LIBRARIES > Block Library.**)

2   Click **Search > By Notecard**

3   Put checks next to the fields you want to
    search (Name, Reference, and Notes).

4   Under **Find at most ___ items** enter a
    number between 1 and 999, or leave it at the
    default which is 50.

5   In the box at the top marked **Find all the
    blocks with this notecard text,** type the word
    or words you want to search by.

6   Click the **Search** button. After the progress
    bar disappears, click **OK**. You will now be
    viewing the Search Results section of
    the Library.

7   Drag the horizontal scrollbar beneath the
    blocks to see all the search results.

8   If you want to use a block from the search,
    click directly on it to select it. Click **Add to
    Sketchbook**. You can add as few or as many
    blocks as you want.

9   Click **Search > By Notecard** again to do
    a new search or click **Close** to return to the
    worktable.

Notes
• You will see more results if you check all 3 fields (Name,
  Reference, and Notes). Or, if you type part of the name
  instead of the full name. For instance, search for "ohio"
  instead of "ohio star."

• If you are searching for blocks and have BlockBase
  installed, be sure to put a check next to Notes. BlockBase
  names are numbers. The earliest known name for the
  block *(not all names)* is in the BlockBase Notes.

• Order is important when you type in more than one
  search word. You will get different results if you type in
  "Sue Sunbonnet" instead of "Sunbonnet Sue."

Searching for Blocks by Category

Each block in the Block Library is marked according to predetermined categories. These categories are grouped into sections: Difficulty & Piecing Info, Events, Holidays, Pieced, and Appliqué.

1   Click **LIBRARIES > Block Library**.

2   Click **Search > By Category**.

3   Click any section to view the categories.

4   **Click the image next to a category name to add the category to the search.** You can add more than one. If you wish to remove a category, click the image next to the category name again, to deselect it.

5   Under **Find at most ___ blocks** enter a number between 1 and 999, or leave it at the default which is 50.

6   Click the **Search** button, then **OK**. You will now be viewing the Search Results section.

7   Drag the horizontal scrollbar beneath the blocks to see all the search results.

8   If you want to use a block from the search, **click directly on the block to select it**. Click **Add to Sketchbook**. You can add as few or as many blocks as you want.

9   Click **Search > By Category** again to perform a new search or click **Close** to return to the worktable.

Notes

- The blocks returned must fit into *all* the categories chosen. You can add up to 20 categories, but your results will be fewer and fewer the more you add.

- If you want to save the search results, consider copying and pasting these blocks into their own style in My Library. See page 144 of the EQ6 User Manual. For instance, if you are a beginning quilter and would like to stick to "Triangles and Rectangles," copy, paste, and save those results into a new library. Then go to that My Library each time you need a block for a new project.

Step 1

Step 2

Step 5

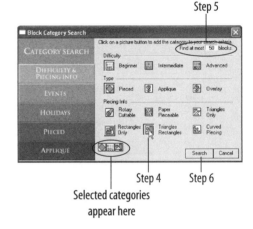

Step 4   Step 6

Selected categories
appear here

Step 6

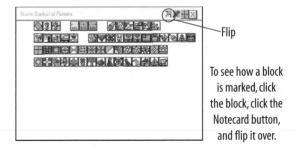

Flip

To see how a block
is marked, click
the block, click the
Notecard button,
and flip it over.

Block Categories

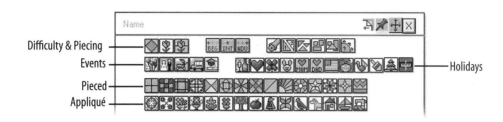

Difficulty & Piecing

Events

Pieced

Appliqué

Holidays

Difficulty & Piecing Info

 Pieced

 Beginner

Rotary Cuttable

Rectangles Only

Appliqué

Intermediate

Paper Pieceable

Triangles Rectangles Only

Overlay

Advanced

Triangles Only

Curved Piecing

Events

Birthday

First Day of School

Wedding

Graduation

Baby

Holidays

New Year's

Easter

Fourth of July

Hanukkah

Valentine's Day

Mother's Day

Halloween

Christmas

St. Patrick's Day

Father's Day

Thanksgiving

Kwanzaa

Pieced

Four Patch

Five Patch

Maltese Cross

Equal Nine Patch

Four X

Nine X

Unequal Nine Patch

Square in a Square

Two-Patch Patterns

Fans

 Eight-Point Stars

 Wheels

 Other Stars

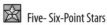 Five- Six-Point Stars

 Borders

Appliqué

 Wreaths

 Containers

 Trees

 Butterflies

Houses Buildings

Four Eight Elements

Leaves

Fruits Vegetables

Birds

Boats

Bouquets

Flowers

People

Animals

Hobbies

Index

Numbers

"88" (Rita Denenberg) 168
0 180
1 180
12 Point Star 52
13-leaf Stem 192
19th-century Leaves 134
1 Big and Little Diamond 229
1 Big and Little Point In 229
1 Big and Little Point Out 229
1 Diamond 229
1 Double Diamond 229
1 Drop Big and Little Diamond 229
1 Drop Diamond 229
1 Drop Double Diamond 229
1 Point In 229
1 Point Out 229
2 180
2 Big and Little Diamonds 230
2 Big and Little Points In 230
2 Big and Little Points Out 230
2 Diamonds 229
2 Double Diamonds 230
2 Drop Big and Little Diamonds 230
2 Drop Diamonds 229
2 Drop Double Diamonds 230
2 Points In 230
2 Points Out 230
3 180
3's 72
3-D 76
3-D Zig Zag Border 239
3 Big and Little Diamonds 230
3 Big and Little Points In 230
3 Big and Little Points Out 230
3 Blade Dresden Fan 18
3 Blade Dresden Flower Fan 18
3 Blade Dresden Plate 22
3 Blade Large Center Dresden Fan 19
3 Blade Large Center Dresden Plate 22
3 Blade Small Center Dresden Fan 19
3 Blade Small Center Dresden Plate 22
3 Diamonds 230
3 Double Diamonds 230
3 Drop Big and Little Diamonds 230
3 Drop Diamonds 230
3 Drop Double Diamonds 230

3 Log Cabin 115
3 Petal Dresden Fan 19
3 Petal Dresden Flower Fan 19
3 Petal Dresden Plate 23
3 Petal Large Center Dresden Fan 20
3 Petal Large Center Dresden Plate 23
3 Petal Small Center Dresden Fan 20
3 Petal Small Center Dresden Plate 23
3 Points In 230
3 Points Out 230
4 180
4-Patch Chain 65
4-Patch Snowball 65
4 Big and Little Diamonds 230
4 Big and Little Points In 231
4 Big and Little Points Out 231
4 Blade Dresden Fan 18
4 Blade Dresden Flower Fan 18
4 Blade Dresden Plate 22
4 Blade Large Center Dresden Fan 19
4 Blade Large Center Dresden Plate 22
4 Blade Small Center Dresden Fan 19
4 Blade Small Center Dresden Plate 22
4 Diamonds 230
4 Double Diamonds 230
4 Drop Big and Little Diamonds 230
4 Drop Diamonds 230
4 Drop Double Diamonds 230
4 Log Cabin 115
4 Petal Dresden Fan 19
4 Petal Dresden Flower Fan 19
4 Petal Dresden Plate 23
4 Petal Large Center Dresden Fan 20
4 Petal Large Center Dresden Plate 23
4 Petal Small Center Dresden Fan 20
4 Petal Small Center Dresden Plate 23
4 Points In 231
4 Points Out 231
5 180
5-Grid Chain 13
5 Big and Little Diamonds 231
5 Big and Little Points In 231
5 Big and Little Points Out 231
5 Blade Dresden Fan 18
5 Blade Dresden Flower Fan 18
5 Blade Dresden Plate 22
5 Blade Large Center Dresden Fan 19
5 Blade Large Center Dresden Plate 22
5 Blade Small Center Dresden Fan 19
5 Blade Small Center Dresden Plate 22
5 Diamonds 231
5 Double Diamonds 231
5 Drop Big and Little Diamonds 231

5 Drop Diamonds 231
5 Drop Double Diamonds 231
5 Log Cabin 115
5 Petal Dresden Fan 20
5 Petal Dresden Flower Fan 19
5 Petal Dresden Plate 23
5 Petal Large Center Dresden Fan 20
5 Petal Large Center Dresden Plate 23
5 Petal Small Center Dresden Fan 20
5 Petal Small Center Dresden Plate 23
5 Points In 231
5 Points Out 231
6 180
6-Grid Chain 13
6 Big and Little Diamonds 231
6 Big and Little Points In 231
6 Big and Little Points Out 231
6 Blade Dresden Fan 18
6 Blade Dresden Flower Fan 18
6 Blade Dresden Plate 22
6 Blade Large Center Dresden Fan 19
6 Blade Large Center Dresden Plate 22
6 Blade Small Center Dresden Fan 19
6 Blade Small Center Dresden Plate 22
6 Diamonds 231
6 Double Diamonds 231
6 Drop Big and Little Diamonds 231
6 Drop Diamonds 231
6 Drop Double Diamonds 231
6 Log Cabin 115
6 Petal Dresden Fan 20
6 Petal Dresden Flower Fan 19
6 Petal Dresden Plate 23
6 Petal Large Center Dresden Fan 20
6 Petal Large Center Dresden Plate 23
6 Petal Small Center Dresden Fan 20
6 Petal Small Center Dresden Plate 23
6 Points In 231
6 Points Out 231
7 180
7's 72
7-Grid Chain 13
7 Big and Little Diamonds 232
7 Big and Little Points In 232
7 Big and Little Points Out 232
7 Blade Dresden Fan 18
7 Blade Dresden Flower Fan 18
7 Blade Dresden Plate 22
7 Blade Large Center Dresden Fan 19
7 Blade Large Center Dresden Plate 22
7 Blade Small Center Dresden Fan 19
7 Blade Small Center Dresden Plate 22
7 Diamonds 232

7 Double Diamonds *232*
7 Drop Big and Little Diamonds *232*
7 Drop Diamonds *232*
7 Drop Double Diamonds *232*
7 Log Cabin *115*
7 Petal Dresden Fan *20*
7 Petal Dresden Flower Fan *19*
7 Petal Dresden Plate *23*
7 Petal Large Center Dresden Fan *20*
7 Petal Large Center Dresden Plate *23*
7 Petal Small Center Dresden Fan *20*
7 Petal Small Center Dresden Plate *23*
7 Points In *232*
7 Points Out *232*
8 *180*
8-Grid Chain *13*
8-Grid Chain Variation *13*
8 Blade Dresden Fan *18*
8 Blade Dresden Flower Fan *18*
8 Blade Dresden Plate *22*
8 Blade Large Center Dresden Fan *19*
8 Blade Large Center Dresden Plate *22*
8 Blade Small Center Dresden Fan *19*
8 Blade Small Center Dresden Plate *22*
8 Log Cabin *115*
8 Petal Dresden Fan *20*
8 Petal Dresden Flower Fan *19*
8 Petal Dresden Plate *23*
8 Petal Large Center Dresden Fan *20*
8 Petal Large Center Dresden Plate *23*
8 Petal Small Center Dresden Fan *20*
8 Petal Small Center Dresden Plate *23*
9 *180*
9-Patch *65*
9-Patch Chain *65*
9-Patch Flower *216*
9-Patch Snowball *65*
9 Log Cabin *115*

A

A *7, 8, 178*
a *178*
A (Foundation-Pieced Alphabet) *94*
a (Foundation-Pieced Alphabet) *93*
a acute (Foundation-Pieced Alphabet) *96*
a circumflex (Foundation-Pieced Alphabet) *96*
A Flock *217*
a grave (Foundation-Pieced Alphabet) *96*
A is for Apple *214*
a ring (Foundation-Pieced Alphabet) *96*
A Snowflake *37*
a tilde (Foundation-Pieced Alphabet) *96*

a umlaut (Foundation-Pieced Alphabet) *96*
Abyssinian Cat *149*
Adirondack Baskets *59*
Aevi (Shiba Inu) *157*
ae diphthong (Foundation-Pieced Alphabet) *96*
African Violets *106*
Airways *47*
Alabama Album Quilt *133*
Alabama Beauty *45*
Alabama Variation *13*
Album *36, 111*
Album-Churn Dash Variation *6*
Album-Variable Star *6*
Album-Variable Star II *6*
Album-Variable Star III *6*
Album-Variable Star IV *6*
Album-Variable Star V *6*
Album-Variable Star VI *6*
Album 2 *111*
Album Block *6*
Album Block II *6*
Album Block III *6*
Album Block IV *6*
Album Block V *6*
Album Block VI *6*
Album Block VII *6*
Album Block VIII *6*
Album Quilt *31*
Aleph © Debbie Sichel *92*
Algeria *84*
Alhambra Tile *172*
Alligator *97*
All Hallows *41*
All Kinds *35*
Almost Amish Basket *59*
Alpha (Greek Alphabet) *90*
alpha (Greek Alphabet) *90*
Alpine Flower *65, 70*
Amanda *142*
Amaryllis Bulb *65*
Ambulance *100*
American Chain *110*
American Star *139, 188*
Amish Basket *59*
Ampersand *180*
Andrea's Blanket *79*
Andrea's Fancy *215*
Andrea's LeMoyne *27*
Andrew *142*
Anemones (quarter design) *161*
Angel *112*
Angel (Rita Denenberg) *153*
Angel Fish *159, 184*

Angel with Candle *153*
Angel with Harp *152*
Angled Purse *169*
Ann's House *69*
Ann's Angel *153*
Ann's Garden Wreath *156*
Another Elf Tree *110*
Another Tiny Tree *110*
Anthurium *106*
Antique Appliqué Leaf *193*
Antique Appliqué Leaves *192*
Antique Appliqué Maple *192*
Antique Appliqué Oak *192*
Antique Appliqué Oak *192*
Antique Baltimore Album House *140*
Antique Bird *181*
Antique Birdcage (Rita Denenberg) *163*
Antique Dove *131, 181*
Antique Eagle *131*
Antique Eagle 2 *132*
Antique Flower Scroll *229*
Antique Flower Scroll 2 *229*
Antique Leaf Wreath *197*
Antique Redbird *131*
Antique Tulips *133*
Antique Tulip Cross *133*
Antique Woodpecker *131*
Apple *108, 156, 163, 188*
Apple Tree *125, 194, 217*
Apple Tree 2 *125*
Apricot *163*
April Autograph *58*
Arabesque *172, 209*
Arabia *172*
Arbor Window *18*
Argentina *84*
Argyle *210*
Argyle Socks *70*
Arkansas Snowflake *41, 50*
Arkansas Traveler *33*
Armenia *84*
Around the World *24*
Arrowheads *39*
Art Square *17*
Asparagus *108*
Aster *104, 106*
Attic Flag *83*
Attic Window *14, 40, 51*
August Autograph *58*
August Sun *80*
Aunt Addie's Album *53*
Aunt Dinah *42*
Aunt Eliza's Star *42*

Aunt Malvernia's Chain Variation *41*
Aunt Melvernia's Chain *34*
Australia *84*
Austria *84*
Autumn Cross Patch *218*
Ayin © Debbie Sichel *93*

B

B *7, 8, 178*
b *178*
B (Foundation-Pieced Alphabet) *94*
b (Foundation-Pieced Alphabet) *93*
B is for Bear *214*
Baby's First Birthday *150*
Baby Aster *55*
Baby Bath *151*
Baby Bottle *102*
Baby Rattle *102*
Baby Stroller *102*
Baby with Blocks *150*
Bachelor's Button *106*
Ball *123, 195*
Ballerina *151*
Balloons *194*
Baltimore *69*
Baltimore Album Leaf *192*
Baltimore Block *134*
Bamboo Fence Border *226*
Banana *163*
Bananas *108*
Banner *208*
Barbados *84*
Barbershop Baskets *59*
Barn Friends *217*
Baron VanBarker (Daschund) *157*
Baseball *24, 170, 195*
Baseball (Rita Denenberg) *170*
Baseball Cap (Rita Denenberg) *171, 195*
Bashful Sam *143, 196*
Basic 4X *34*
Basic New York Beauty *117*
Basket *12, 98, 99*
Basketball *170, 195*
Basketball Hoop (Rita Denenberg) *170, 195*
Basket of Flowers *12*
Basket of Lilies *12*
Basket on the Table *99*
Basket Pinwheel *59*
Basket Variation *137*
Basket with Handles *12, 130*
Basket with Ribbon *130*
Basket with Trim *98*

Bass Clef *168*
Bass Staff *168*
Bat's Wings *36*
Bathtub Boat *67*
Baton Rouge Block *36*
Bats in Web (Rita Denenberg) *167*
Beach 1 *100*
Beach 2 *100*
Beans (Pug) *158*
Bear *97*
Bear's Paw *15*
Bear and a Tree *114*
Bear Head *109*
Bee *148*
Beet *156, 189*
Beetle *148*
Beggar Block *41*
Belgium *84*
Belize *85*
Bell *152*
Bells with Holly *152*
Belt Buckle *74*
Bel Geddes *75*
Bendera (Kwanzaa Flag) *166*
Bermuda *85*
Berry Basket *59, 60*
Berry Scroll *228*
Bessie *141*
Beta (Greek Alphabet) *90*
beta (Greek Alphabet) *90*
Bettina's Star *72*
Bet © Debbie Sichel *92*
Big & Little Trees *82*
Big Basket *99*
Big Bass (Rita Denenberg) *167*
Big Bird House *109*
Big Dipper *157, 190*
Big Pine *82*
Big Striped Basket *99*
Bike *174*
Biker (Rita Denenberg) *155*
Bird *155, 182*
Bird's Eye View *54*
Bird's Nest *36*
Bird's Nest *30*
Birdhouse *155, 182*
Birds and Star *27*
Birds in the Air *14*
Birds in the Pine *82*
Birds on Bough *142*
Birds on Branch Silhouette *193*
Bird 2 *155, 182*
Bird 3 *155*

Bird and Bell Toy *151*
Bird from Album Quilt *131, 181*
Bird from Album Quilt 2 *131, 181*
Bird Head *109*
Bird House *67*
Bird in Flight *131, 181*
Bird in the Buds *163, 182*
Bird of Paradise *41*
Bird on a Fence *155*
Bird on House *181*
Bird Sitting *131*
Bird Standing *131*
Bird Standing 2 *131*
Bird Standing 3 *131*
Bird with Tail Feathers *131*
Birthday Cake *101*
Birthday Party *67*
Birthday Toys and Ribbon *151*
Bison *97*
Bits & Pieces *79*
Black-Eyed Susan *78, 186, 187*
Black-eyed Susan *106*
Black-Eyed Susans *160*
Black Cat (Rita Denenberg) *167*
Black Tulip *136*
Blazing Star *26, 37*
Blazing Star 2 *37*
Bleeding Heart (Rita Denenberg) *161*
Bleeding Heart from Grandma Dexter *136*
Blockade *33*
Blocks in a Box *110*
Blocks in a Box Variation *110*
Blocks in a Box Variation 2 *110*
Blooming Orchid *216*
Blossom *64*
Blossoms *185, 206*
Blossoms Stencil *205*
Blossom and Berries *186*
Bluebell *105*
Bluebell Star *215*
Blueberries *163*
Blueberry Pie *78*
Bluebird by Nancy Cabot, 1944 *131, 181*
Bluebird in Flight *131, 181*
Bluebird on Branch *155, 181*
Bluebird Scroll *229*
Blue Boutonnieres *33*
Blue Buds *162*
Blue Buds (quarter design) *161*
Blue Chains *13*
Blue Heron *97*
Blue Shirt *81*
Blue Spruce *82, 83*

Blue Spruce 2 *83*
Boat *47, 100*
Boise *34*
Bolt of Fabric *175*
Bonnet Baby Boy from McKim Studios *143*
Bonnet Baby Girl from McKim Studios *143*
Boot with Buttons *169*
Boot with Laces *169*
Bored Meeting *81*
Bottle Brush *134*
Bouquet *160, 162*
Bouquet from Album Quilt *137*
Bowling Ball (Rita Denenberg) *170, 195*
Bowling Green *69*
Bowling Pin (Rita Denenberg) *170, 195*
Bowl of Fruit *48, 142*
Bowl on Striped Cloth *99*
Bow Tie *14, 51*
Box-in-a-Box *201*
Box-in-a-Box 2 *201*
Box-in-a-Box 3 *201*
Box-in-a-Box 4 *201*
Box-in-a-Box 5 *201*
Box-in-a-Box 6 *202*
Box-in-a-Box 7 *202*
Box-in-a-Box Variation *51*
Boxed Diagonals 1 *201*
Boxed Diagonals 2 *201*
Boxed Diagonals 3 *201*
Boxed Diagonals 4 *201*
Boxed Diagonals 5 *201*
Boxed Star *27*
Boxed Tree *124*
Boxing Gloves (Rita Denenberg) *171, 195*
Box Elder *191*
Boy and Butterfly *151*
Boy and Dog *151*
Boy Walking a Dog *157*
Boy with Cake *151*
Boy with Train *151*
Bradley *75*
Braid Wreath *211*
Brazil *85*
Bread Basket *130*
Brick Path Medallion *56*
Brittany Basket *59*
Brocade Scrollwork *229*
Broken Band Variation *111*
Broken Dishes *14, 32*
Broken Heart *165*
Broken Sash Strip *66*
Broken Sash Strip 2 *66*
Broken Sash Strip 3 *66*

Broken Wheel *41*
Brontosaurus *173*
Brooklyn *69*
Brownstones *113*
Brunei *85*
Bubbles Fish *159, 184*
Bucket and Shovel *100*
Buckle Closure Purse *169*
Buckwheat *34, 35*
Buds and Ribbons *64*
Buds in a Circle *197*
Bud and Berries *185*
Bud Block *134*
Bud Fish *159, 183*
Bullseye *203*
Bumble Bee *148*
Bunny *64, 158*
Bunny with Egg (Rita Denenberg) *159*
Bunny with Tulip (Rita Denenberg) *151*
Burmese Cat *149*
Burnham *75*
Butterflies *156, 183*
Butterflies 2 *183*
Butterflies and Blossom *156, 183*
Butterflies in Flight *132, 133, 183*
Butterfly *47, 48, 64, 143, 156, 182*
Butterfly (Judy Vigiletti) *68*
Butterfly 2 *132, 156, 182*
Butterfly 3 *132, 156, 182*
Butterfly 4 *132, 156, 183*
Butterfly and Flower *133*
Butterfly Fan *63*
Butterfly from 1936 *132, 183*
Butterfly from 30s Quilt *132, 182*
Butterfly from 40s Quilt *132*
Butterfly from Baltimore Album *132, 182*
Butterfly from Tennessee Quilt *132*
Butterfly Ring *132*
Butterfly Ring 2 *132*
Butterfly Star *218*
Butterfly Too (Judy Vigiletti) *68*
Butterfly with Curling Antennae *132*
Butterfly with Scalloped Wings *132, 183*
Button *73*
Button up Purse *169*
Byzantium *172*

C

C *7, 8, 178*
c *178*
C (Foundation-Pieced Alphabet) *95*
c (Foundation-Pieced Alphabet) *93*

c cedilla (Foundation-Pieced Alphabet) *96*
C is for Cat *214*
Cabbage Rose Wreath *141*
Cabin *114*
Cactus Bud *40*
Cake *150*
Cake Stand *48*
Calico Cartoon Cat *149*
Calico Puzzle *40*
California Friendship Star *28*
Camel *97*
Canada *85*
Candle *112, 153*
Candle and Holder *153*
Candle and Holly *153*
Candy Canes *79, 152*
Canteloupe *163*
Capital T *37*
Captured Feathers *218*
Car *174*
Cardinal *97, 155, 182*
Card Basket *43*
Card Trick *40*
Carnation *185*
Carnations in Bloom *138*
Carnation (Rita Denenberg) *161*
Carnation Cross *133*
Carousel Horse (Rita Denenberg) *174*
Carpenter's Wheel *27, 38*
Carpenter's Wheel 2 *38*
Carpie Fish *159, 184*
Carrie Nation Quilt *33*
Carrot *108, 156, 189*
Carrying Basket *130*
Cartoon Cat Silhouette *149*
Cartoon Dog *158*
Cartoon Puppy *158*
Car Front *100*
Castle Wall *55*
Cat *64, 149*
Cat's Tails *70*
Cats and Mice *54*
Cat Head *109*
Cat Silhouette *193*
Cat with Ball Silhouette *149*
CD *175*
Celtic Circle *202*
Celtic Hearts *165*
Celtic Hearts with Leaves *165*
Celtic Interweave *202*
Celtic Patch *173*
Celtic Patch 2 *173*
Celtic Patch 3 *173*

252

Celtic Patch 4 *173*
Celtic Patch 5 *173*
Celtic Patch 6 *173*
Celtic Patch 7 *173*
Celtic Rope *202*
Celtic Squares and Loops *202*
Celtic Squares and Loops 2 *202*
Celtic Squares and Loops 3 *202*
Center Diamond Variation *51*
Ceramic Planter *105*
Chain 1 *65*
Chain and Knot Variation *13*
Chair and Towel *100*
Chair and Umbrella *99*
Chariot Wheel *54*
Charlotte *142*
Charm Basket *60*
Checked Arc Beauty *117*
Checked Arc Beauty 2 *117*
Checked Arc Beauty 3 *117*
Checked Arc Beauty 4 *117*
Checked X *77*
Checkerboard *34*
Checkerboard Basket *59*
Checkerboard Medallion *55*
Check and Triangle Border *236*
Check and Triangle Border 2 *236*
Check and Triangle Border 3 *236*
Check and Triangle Border 4 *236*
Check and Triangle Corner *236*
Check and Triangle Corner 2 *236*
Check and Triangle Corner 3 *236*
Check and Triangle Corner 4 *236*
Check Border 1A *222*
Check Border 1B *222*
Check Border 2A *222*
Check Border 2B *222*
Check Border 3 *222*
Check Border 4A *222*
Check Border 4B *222*
Check Border 5 *222*
Check Border 6 *222*
Check Border 7 *222*
Check Border 8A *223*
Check Border 8B *223*
Check Border 9 *223*
Check Corner 1A *222*
Check Corner 1B *222*
Check Corner 2A *222*
Check Corner 2B *222*
Check Corner 3 *222*
Check Corner 4A *222*
Check Corner 4B *222*

Check Corner 6 *222*
Check Corner 7 *223*
Check Corner 8A *223*
Check Corner 8B *223*
Check Corner 9 *223*
Cherries *163, 189*
Cherry Wreath *145*
Chet © Debbie Sichel *92*
Chevrons & Strips Border *237*
Chevrons & Strips Corner *237*
Chevrons and Stripes Border *238*
Chevrons and Stripes Corner *238*
Cheyenne Star *72*
Cheyenne Star Variation *72*
Chicago *69*
Chicago Star *36, 52*
Chick *181*
Chick (Rita Denenberg) *158*
Children's Delight *30*
Chile *85*
China *85*
China Doll *123*
China Doll (Rita Denenberg) *174*
Chinese Lanterns *44*
Chips and Whetstones *15*
Chi (Greek Alphabet) *91*
chi (Greek Alphabet) *92*
Chloe Fish *159, 183*
Christina *142*
Christmas Cactus *145*
Christmas Goose *154*
Christmas Morning *217*
Christmas Pine *82*
Christmas Snowflake *209*
Christmas Stocking (Rita Denenberg) *154*
Christmas Tree *112, 125, 153*
Christmas Tree (Rita Denenberg) *153*
Christ Child (Rita Denenberg) *154*
Chrysanthemum *106, 136*
Church with Steeple *113*
Churn Dash *15*
Circle-in-a-Circle *203*
Circle-in-a-Circle 2 *203*
Circled Star *29*
Circle Rose *134, 187*
Circle Rose 2 *134*
Circle Star *16*
Circle Wreath *212*
City Bus *100*
Clamshell *45, 203*
Clarinet (Rita Denenberg) *168*
Classic Dresden Bladed Plate *22*
Classic Dresden Plate *23*

Classic Urn *144*
Clay's Choice *14, 32*
Clematis *136*
Cleopatra's Puzzle *24*
Cloud *156, 190*
Clover *203*
Clovers and Spades *133*
Clown *31*
Clown's Choice *41*
Clown Doll *174*
Clustered Square Medallion *55*
Cock's Comb *34*
Cock's Comb and Currants *136*
Coffin Star *17, 51*
Coin Purse *169*
Collie *64*
Colonial Girl *196*
Colonial Lady *143*
Columbia *29, 85*
Comb *134*
Combed Swag Border *234*
Comb and Currants Scroll *229*
Comet *70*
Coming Home (Rita Denenberg) *154*
Comma *180*
Compact Car *101*
Compass Points *16*
Compass Star *15*
Complex Crazy 1 *102*
Complex Crazy 10 *102*
Complex Crazy 11 *102*
Complex Crazy 12 *102*
Complex Crazy 13 *103*
Complex Crazy 14 *103*
Complex Crazy 2 *102*
Complex Crazy 3 *102*
Complex Crazy 4 *102*
Complex Crazy 5 *102*
Complex Crazy 6 *102*
Complex Crazy 7 *102*
Complex Crazy 8 *102*
Complex Crazy 9 *102*
Complex Maple Leaf *115*
Computer Monitor *175*
Computer Tower *176*
Concentric Orchids Hawaiian Appliqué *164*
Condo *69*
Coneflower *187*
Coneflower 2 *187*
Connecticut Star Variation *38*
Constellation Patch *218*
Contemporary House 1 *113*
Contemporary House 2 *113*

Continuous Greek Key *200*
Continuous Line Bells *201*
Continuous Line Diamonds *200*
Continuous Line Double Ovals *200*
Continuous Line Fall *200*
Continuous Line Feathers *200*
Continuous Line Fish *200*
Continuous Line Flowers *200*
Continuous Line Hearts *200*
Continuous Line Houses *200*
Continuous Line Loops *200*
Continuous Line Maple Leaves *201*
Continuous Line Moon & Stars *201*
Continuous Line Ovals *200*
Continuous Line Sawtooth *200*
Continuous Line Spring *200*
Continuous Line Stars *200*
Continuous Line Summer *200*
Continuous Line Waves *200*
Continuous Line Winter *200*
Contrary Wife *17, 40*
Contrary Wife Variation *17*
Convertible *100*
Cook Islands *85*
Cool Fan *74*
Cool Mint Candy *78*
Corgi *157*
Corn *108*
Cornered Star *28*
Corner Hearts *165*
Cornucopia *44, 167*
Corn and Beans *15*
Corn on the Cob *189*
Cosmos Wreath *197*
Costa Rica *85*
Costume Jewelry *74*
Country Cottage *68*
Country Crown *76*
Country Farm *43*
Country Lawyer *81*
Courthouse *113*
Courthouse Stars *71*
Courthouse Steps *116*
Courthouse Steps 2 *117*
Courtyard *16*
Cow *97, 142, 155, 194*
Cowboy Shirt *81*
Cowboy Sue *143*
Cow Silhouette *193*
Coxcomb in Pot *140, 188*
Coxey's Camp *17, 25*
Crab *64*
Crab Apple *82*

Cracker *111*
Crane *131*
Crazy 1 *103*
Crazy 10 *104*
Crazy 11 *104*
Crazy 12 *104*
Crazy 13 *104*
Crazy 14 *104*
Crazy 15 *104*
Crazy 16 *104*
Crazy 17 *104*
Crazy 18 *104*
Crazy 19 *104*
Crazy 2 *103*
Crazy 20 *104*
Crazy 3 *103*
Crazy 4 *103*
Crazy 5 *103*
Crazy 6 *103*
Crazy 7 *103*
Crazy 8 *103*
Crazy 9 *104*
Crazy Fan 1 *103*
Crazy Fan 2 *103*
Crazy Fan 3 *103*
Crazy Fan 4 *103*
Crazy Fan 5 *103*
Crazy Fan 6 *103*
Crazy Fan 7 *103*
Crazy Fan 8 *103*
Crazy Geese 1 *102*
Crazy Geese 2 *102*
Crazy Geese 3 *102*
Crazy Geese 4 *102*
Crazy House *31*
Crazy Log Cabin *116*
Crepe Myrtle *106*
Crescent Moon *157*
Criss-Cross Medallion *56*
Criss Cross Border *225*
Criss Cross Corner *225*
Criss Cross Variation *35*
Croatia *85*
Crocodile *97*
Crocus *105*
Crossed Canoes *25*
Crosses and Star *36*
Crossing Branches *134*
Crossing Diagonals *210*
Crossing Diagonals 2 *210*
Crossing Feathers *204*
Crossing Hearts *166*
Crossing Ribbons *208*

Crossing Roses *133*
Crossing Squares *201*
Crossing Squares 2 *201*
Crossing Winds *76*
Cross 1 *60*
Cross 10 *60*
Cross 11 *60*
Cross 12 *60*
Cross 13 *61*
Cross 14 *61*
Cross 15 *61*
Cross 16 *61*
Cross 2 *60*
Cross 3 *60*
Cross 4 *60*
Cross 5 *60*
Cross 6 *60*
Cross 7 *60*
Cross 8 *60*
Cross 9 *60*
Cross and Crown *15, 30*
Cross Roads *33, 42*
Cross within Cross *36*
Cross with a Cross *17*
Cross with Cross Autograph *58*
Cross X *66*
Crown of Thorns *32*
Crystal Snowflake *209*
Cupid *166*
Curled Leaf *193*
Curled Leaf Wreath *197*
Curly Flower with Center *156*
Curved-handle Basket *98*
Curved Path Border *224*
Curved Path Corner *224*
Cutout Snowflake *209*
Cut Glass Dish *36*
Czech Republic *85*

D

D *7, 8, 178*
d *178*
D (Foundation-Pieced Alphabet) *95*
d (Foundation-Pieced Alphabet) *93*
D is for Dog *214*
Dad's Bow Tie *34*
Daffodil *105, 106, 185, 205*
Daffodil (Rita Denenberg) *161*
Daffodil Leaves *105*
Daffodil Ring *65*
Dahlia *161*
Daisy *104, 162, 185, 186*

Daisy Chain 206
Daisy Cluster 197
Daisy Petal Fan 63
Daisy Star 15
Daisy Swag Border 234
Daisy Wreath 145
Dakota Star 67
Dalet © Debbie Sichel 92
Darting Birds 40
David Star (Rita Denenberg) 166
Day Lilies 139
Day Lily 39
Dean's Sunflower Sun 80
December Autograph 58
Decorative Vase 144
Deer 142
Deer and a Tree 114
Deer Silhouette 193
Deinonychus 174
Delectable Mountains Border 239
Delectable Mountains Corner 239
Delta (Greek Alphabet) 90
delta (Greek Alphabet) 90
Democratic People's Republic of Korea 86
Denmark 85
Detroit 69
Devil's Puzzle 36
Diagonal Lines 210
Diagonal Strips 50, 110
Diagonal Strips 2 50, 110
Diamond-in-Square Log Cabin 116
Diamond-in-the-Tree 83
Diamonds 202
Diamonds & Triangles Border 238
Diamonds & Triangles Corner 238
Diamonds 2 202
Diamonds and Strips Border 237
Diamonds and Strips Corner 237
Diamonds in Squares 56
Diamond Border 236
Diamond Border 2 236
Diamond Bracelet 70
Diamond Center Log Cabin 116
Diamond Corner 236
Diamond Corner 2 236
Diamond Diane 78
Diamond Diane's Fan 63
Diamond Fan 3 62
Diamond Fan 4 62
Diamond Fan 5 62
Diamond Fan 6 62
Diamond Fan 7 62
Diamond Fan 8 63

Diamond Flower 218
Diamond Grid 210
Diamond in Square Strips Border 238
Diamond in Square Strips Corner 238
Diamond in the Square 16, 51, 111
Diamond Ring 70
Diamond Star 30, 73, 77
Diamond Sun 80
Diamond Wreath 212
Divided Star 30
Dizzy Spinner 78
Dog 142
Dogtooth Violet 33
Dog Before Nap 158
Dog Head 109
Dog Silhouette 157, 193
Dog Silhouette 2 194
Dog with Ball 158
Dolphins at Play Hawaiian Appliqué 164
Domino 37
Doris' Delight 43
Dots 24
Dotted Dress 155
Double-Baskets 59
Double-Crossed Hearts 207
Double-Decker Bus 101
Double-Heart Ring 206
Double-Plume Medallion 204
Double Cross 17
Double Diamonds Border 237
Double Diamonds Border 2 238
Double Diamonds Corner 238
Double Diamonds Corner 2 238
Double Four Patch 12
Double Grapes 241
Double Hearts 165
Double Maltese 2 39
Double Maltese 3 39
Double Maltese 3 Variation 39
Double Maltese 4 39
Double Maltese 4 Variation 39
Double Monkey Wrench 41, 50
Double Nine Patch 12, 40
Double Pickle Dish - 4 Points 46
Double Pickle Dish - 5 Points 46
Double Pickle Dish - 7 Points 46
Double Pickle Dish Side - 4 Points 46
Double Pickle Dish Side - 5 Points 46
Double Pickle Dish Side - 7 Points 46
Double Pinwheel Whirls 25, 67
Double Plume 204
Double Sawtooth Border 236
Double Sawtooth Corner 236

Double Scallop 211
Double Scalloped Swag Border 234
Double Star 53
Double Star Variation 52
Double Tassle Swag Border 234
Double Tulip 105, 185
Double Wave 210
Double Wedding Ring 14
Double Wedding Ring - 4 Segments 46
Double Wedding Ring - 5 Segments 46
Double Wedding Ring - 7 Segments 46
Double Wedding Ring Side - 4 Segments 46
Double Wedding Ring Side - 5 Segments 46
Double Wedding Ring Side - 7 Segments 46
Double Windmill 44
Double X, No.1 36
Double X, No.2 37
Double X, No.3 37
Double X, No.4 37
Double Y Border 225
Double Y Corner 225
Double Z 36
Dove 24, 153
Doves 131
Dove at the Window 43
Dove Corner Block (Rita Denenberg) 150
Dove in Flight 182
Dove Ornament 152
Downing 75
Dozen-leaf Stem 192
Dozen-leaf Stem 2 192
Dozen-leaf Stem 3 192
Dozen Hearts 206
Dreidel (Rita Denenberg) 166
Dreidel © Debbie Sichel 112
Dresden Basket 48
Dresden Bladed Flower 22
Dresden Flower 23
Dress on a Clothesline 155
Dress with Buttons 155
Dreyfuss 75
Drum 152
Drum (Rita Denenberg) 168
Drum and Sticks 168
Drunkard's Path Border 223
Drunkard's Path Border 2 224
Drunkard's Path Corner 223
Drunkard's Path Corner 2 224
Drunkard's Path 24
Drunkard's Path Variation 24
Drunkard's Pinwheel 24
Duck 154, 182
Duckling 154, 182

Duckling in Shell *158*
Duck 2 *154, 182*
Duck and Ducklings *30*
Duck Pull-toy *174*
Dunce Caps *70*
Dutchman's Puzzle *34*
Dutch Boat *48*
Dutch Girl *143*
Dutch Mill *48*
Dutch Rose *27*
Dutch Tulip *138*

E

E *7, 9, 178*
e *178*
E (Foundation-Pieced Alphabet) *95*
e (Foundation-Pieced Alphabet) *94*
e acute (Foundation-Pieced Alphabet) *96*
e circumflex (Foundation-Pieced Alphabet) *96*
e grave (Foundation-Pieced Alphabet) *96*
E is for Egg *214*
e umlaut (Foundation-Pieced Alphabet) *96*
E (Foundation-Pieced Alphabet) *95*
e (Foundation-Pieced Alphabet) *94*
e acute (Foundation-Pieced Alphabet) *96*
e circumflex (Foundation-Pieced Alphabet) *96*
e grave (Foundation-Pieced Alphabet) *96*
E is for Egg *214*
e umlaut (Foundation-Pieced Alphabet) *96*
Eagle *143, 181, 188*
Eagle Silhouette *193*
Eagle Silhouette 2 *193*
Eagle with Berries *139, 188*
Eagle with Talons *142*
Eames *75*
Early Colonial Cottage *69*
Easter Basket *59*
Easter Basket (Rita Denenberg) *159*
Easter Egg *159*
Easter Egg (Rita Denenberg) *158*
Easter Egg 1 *112*
Easter Egg 2 *112*
Easter Egg 2 (Rita Denenberg) *158*
Easter Egg 3 *112*
Easter Lily (Rita Denenberg) *159*
Easter Rabbit 1 (Rita Denenberg) *158*
Easter Rabbit 2 (Rita Denenberg) *158*
Easter Rabbit 3 (Rita Denenberg) *158*
Eastlake *75*
Easy Leaf *114*
Eccentric Star *40, 50*
Eccentric Star 2 *40*

Eccentric Star 3 *40*
Economy *65*
Economy 2 *66*
Economy Patch *16, 51, 111, 127*
Ecuador *85*
Edward Scissortail Fish *159, 183*
Eggplant *108, 156, 189*
Egypt *85*
Eight *8, 10*
Eight-Pointed Star *43, 50*
Eight-Pointed Star Variation *43*
Eight Blades *54*
Eight Hands Around *53*
Eight Hearts *165*
Eight Point Star (PatchDraw) *26*
Electric Fan *66, 70, 73*
Elephant *64, 97*
Elephant Toy *151*
Eleven-leaf Stem *192*
Eleven Lines *211*
Elf Asleep *110*
Elf Boat *109*
Elf Cottage *109*
Elf Tree *110*
Elm *191*
Elm 2 *192*
Emerging Star *77*
Emily *142*
English Flower Pot *137*
English Ivy *48*
English Rose *135, 187*
English Rose 2 *135*
Epsilon (Greek Alphabet) *90*
epsilon (Greek Alphabet) *90*
EQ's Stars & Beams *73*
EQ Kaleidoscope Star *73*
EQ Logo *67*
EQ Star *73*
EQ Star 2 *73*
EQ Star 3 *73*
EQ Star 4 *73*
EQ Star 5 *73*
EQ Star 6 *73*
Estonia *85*
Eta (Greek Alphabet) *90*
eta (Greek Alphabet) *90*
eth (Foundation-Pieced Alphabet) *96*
European Union *85*
Evening Sail *217*
Evergreen *82, 124*
Evergreen & Shadow *124*
Evergreen & Shadow 2 *124*
Evergreen 1 *124*

Evergreen 2 *124*
Evergreen 3 *124*
Evergreen 4 *124*
Executive *81*

F

F *7, 9, 178*
f *178*
F (Foundation-Pieced Alphabet) *95*
f (Foundation-Pieced Alphabet) *94*
F is for Fish *214*
Fabric Bolts *68*
Faceted Star *70, 77*
Falling Timbers *24*
Fall Dance *216*
Fall Flowers *217*
Fall Meander *200*
Family Tree (Rita Denenberg) *150*
Fan *61*
Fanblades 2 *62*
Fanblades 3 *62*
Fanblades 4 *62*
Fanblades 5 *62*
Fanblades 6 *62*
Fanblades 7 *62*
Fanblades 8 *62*
Fancy Butterfly from Grandmother Clark *132*
Fancy Fence *79*
Fancy Fruit *217*
Fanned Flowers *218*
Fanned Shoe *170*
Fanny's Fan *31*
Fantasia *218*
Fantasy Flower *187*
Fan 2 *61*
Fan 3 *61*
Fan 4 *62*
Fan 5 *62, 66*
Fan 6 *62*
Fan 7 *62*
Fan 8 *62*
Fan and Stars *218*
Fan Border *224*
Fan Corner *224*
Fan Dance 2 *61*
Fan Dance 3 *61*
Fan Dance 4 *61*
Fan Dance 5 *61*
Fan Dance 6 *61*
Fan Dance 7 *61*
Fan Dance 8 *61*
Fan Dance 9 *61*

Fan Dance Border 224
Fan Dance Corner 224
Fan Flower 53, 63
Fan Rails 71
Fan Vase 144
Fan Weaver 74
Fargo 75
Farm House 113
Fat Cat 64
Fat Quarters Fan 63
Fat Ribbon 208
Fat Ribbon 2 209
Feather 204
Feathered LeMoyne 28
Feathered Star 28
Feathered Star in Star 28
Feathered Sunflower Star 28
Feathers 4 204
Feathers 5 204
Feathers 6 204
Feathers with Heart 204
Feathers with Heart Mirrored 204
Feather (border) 204
Feather (corner) 204
Feather (vertical) 204
Feather Meander 200
Feather Plume with Ovals 204
Feather Ring 204
Feather Star 28
Feather Wreath 212
Feather Wreath 1 205
Feather Wreath 2 205, 212
Feather Wreath 3 205, 212
Feather Wreath 4 205, 212
Feather Wreath 5 205
Feather Wreath with Heart 211
February Autograph 58
Feh © Debbie Sichel 93
Feh Sofeet © Debbie Sichel 93
Fifty-Four-Forty-or-Fight 43
Fiji 85
final sigma (Greek Alphabet) 91
Finland 85
Fins Fish 160, 184
Fir 114
Fireplace at Christmas (Rita Denenberg) 154
Fireworks 77, 78, 167
Fireworks Star 73
Fire Truck 101
First-place Flower 138
First Bloom 217
First Dance 101
Fir Tree 112

Fish (Judy Vigiletti) 68
Fish Tank 216
Fish Too (Judy Vigiletti) 68
Fish Too 2 (Judy Vigiletti) 68
Five 8, 10
Five-Pointed Star 29
Five-Point Star 29
Five Border Medallion 56
Five by Three 42
Five Patch Chain 13, 31
Five Patch Shoo Fly 30
Five Pointed Star 29
Five Spot 42
Five Stars 56
Five Wheels with 12 Spokes 74
Flag 109
Flagstones 35
Flag 1 112
Flag 2 112
Flag in a Box 83
Flag in a Box 2 83
Flag in the Square 83
Flamingo 97
Flash Fish 159, 183
Fleur de Lis 172, 228
Flipped Feathers Wreath 211
Floating Fan 63
Floating Pinwheels 71
Floppy 176
Floral Corner 205
Floral Wreath 65
Floral Wreath from Grandma Dexter 145
Flower 194, 209
Flower-in-the-Box 215
Flowering Hawaiian Appliqué 164
Flowering Ohio Star 216
Flowering Snowball 45, 224
Flowering Wheel 215
Flowers 160
Flowers from Antique Sampler 138
Flowers from Antique Sampler Quilt 136
Flowers from Antique Sampler Quilt 2 136
Flowers in Heart Vase 137
Flowers in Pitcher 137
Flower 2 209
Flower 3 209
Flower 4 209
Flower and Bud Wreath 145
Flower and Leaves 160
Flower Basket 12, 130
Flower from the 30s 186
Flower in the Grass 162
Flower of Christmas from Marie Webster 136, 186

Flower Petals 45, 224
Flower Pot 48, 105, 138, 144, 162
Flower Pot 2 162
Flower Sprig 160
Flower Sprig Star 215
Flower Star 52
Flower Wreath 145, 205
Flower Wreath 2 146
Fluted Urn 144
Flying-X 32
Flying Bird 182
Flying Fist 33
Flying Geese 14, 107
Flying Geese 1 107
Flying Geese 10 107
Flying Geese 11 107
Flying Geese 12 107
Flying Geese 13 107
Flying Geese 14 107
Flying Geese 2 107
Flying Geese 3 107
Flying Geese 4 107
Flying Geese 5 107
Flying Geese 6 107
Flying Geese 7 107
Flying Geese 8 107
Flying Geese 9 107
Flying Geese Tree 125
Flying Goose 107
Flying Goose Variation 107
Flying Home 155
Flying Squares 30
Flying Stars 218
Folded Star 72
Folk Art Bird 131, 181
Folk Art Butterfly 132, 182
Folk Art Flower 140, 186, 188
Folk Art Leaf 192
Folk Art Leaf 2 192
Folk Art Leaf Motif 187
Folk Art Twigs and Heart 228
Folk Bird 139, 181, 187, 188
Folk Oak 192
Folk Tulip 139, 187
Fool's Puzzle 24
Fool's Square 30
Football 170, 195
Football (Rita Denenberg) 170
Football Border 223
Football Corner 223
Football Helmet 195
Football Helmet (Rita Denenberg) 170
Forbidden Fruit Tree 48

Forget-Me-Not Ring *145*
Forget-Me-Not Swag Border *234*
Forget-Me-Not Wreath *145*
Formal Garden Variation *50*
Foundation Pieced Wedding Ring *101*
Foundation Pieced Wedding Ring 2 *101*
Foundation Pieced Wedding Ring 3 *101*
Four *8, 10*
Four-Patch Variation *50*
Four-Patch Variation 2 *50*
Four-Patch Variation 3 *50*
Four Blades *54*
Four Block Star *25*
Four by Three *42*
Four by Two *32*
Four Fans Eight Blades *21*
Four Fans Eight Petals *21*
Four Fans Five Blades *21*
Four Fans Five Petals *21*
Four Fans Four Blades *20, 21*
Four Fans Four Petals *21*
Four Fans Nine Blades *20*
Four Fans Nine Petals *21*
Four Fans Seven Blades *21*
Four Fans Seven Petals *21*
Four Fans Six Blades *21*
Four Fans Six Petals *20, 21*
Four Fans Three Blades *21*
Four Fans Three Petals *20, 21*
Four Fan Beauty *118*
Four Fan Beauty 2 *118*
Four Fan Beauty 3 *118*
Four Fan Corner Star *118*
Four Fan Sash *118*
Four Fan Sash 2 *118*
Four Fan Sash 3 *118*
Four Hearts *165*
Four Hearts 2 *165*
Four Hearts 3 *165*
Four Leaf Clover *45*
Four Little Baskets *12*
Four Off-Side Circles *203*
Four Patch *12, 32, 50*
Four Patch Art Square *17*
Four Patch Circle *54*
Four Patch Corner *239*
Four Patch Variable Stars *54*
Four Patch Variation *33*
Four Radiating Petals *205*
Four Ribbons *208*
Four Stars *38*
Four Stars 2 *38*
Four Stars Bordered *27*

Four Stars Patchwork *27*
Four Stars Patchwork Variation *27*
Four Times Four *18*
Four Times Nine *18*
Four X *50, 66*
Four X Star *30*
Four X Variation *34, 51*
Foxglove *65*
Foxglove Too *65*
Fox & Geese *32*
Fox Head *109*
Framed Appliqué *218*
Framed Christmas Wreath *215*
Framed Nine Patch *13*
Framed Stars *218*
France *85*
Frayed Four Patch *13*
Frayed Sawtooth Star *53*
French Knot Border *224*
French Knot Corner *224*
Friendship Bouquet *44*
Friendship Circle *45*
Friendship Star *14, 40, 43*
Frilly Basket *130*
Frog Went A Courtin' *64*
Fruit Basket *12, 48*
Fruit Bowl Silhouette *193*
Fuller *75*
Full Blown Tulip *44*
Full Blown Tulip Variation *44*

G

G *7, 9, 178*
g *178*
G (Foundation-Pieced Alphabet) *95*
g (Foundation-Pieced Alphabet) *94*
G is for Giraffe *214*
Galaxy *76*
Gameboard Medallion *55*
Game Cocks *31*
Gamma (Greek Alphabet) *90*
gamma (Greek Alphabet) *90*
Gardenia (Rita Denenberg) *161*
Garden Basket Variation *12*
Garden Gate (Rita Denenberg) *163*
Garden of Eden *31*
Garden of Hearts *165*
Garden Patch *13, 43*
Garden Patch Variation *43*
Garden Urn *144*
Garret Windows *33*
Gazebo *150*

Geese and Strips Border *237*
Geese and Strips Border 2 *237*
Geese and Strips Corner *237*
Geese and Strips Corner 2 *237*
Gemstone *70*
Geometric Star *49*
Geometric Star 2 Stripe *49*
Geometric Star 3 Stripe *49*
Geometric Star 4 Stripe *49*
Geometric Star 5 Stripe *49*
Geometric Tree *83*
Georgetown Circle *16*
Georgetown Circle Variation *16*
Georgia *85, 142*
Georgian House 1 *113*
Georgian House 2 *113*
Germany *86*
Ghost (Rita Denenberg) *167*
Giant Dahlia *56*
Gift *152*
Gift Box *111*
Gift Package *150*
Gift with a Bow *111*
Gilbert Fish *160, 184*
Gimel © Debbie Sichel *92*
Gingko *124*
Giraffe *97*
Giraffe Toy *151*
Girl's Favorite *33*
Girl's Favorite (2) *33*
Girl Walking a Dog *157*
Girl with Chicks *151*
Girl with Toy Cat *151*
Glass Sunflower *216*
Gloxinia *187*
Goat *98*
Goldie Fish *159, 183*
Golfball (Rita Denenberg) *170*
Golf Ball (Rita Denenberg) *195*
Gone Fishin' (Rita Denenberg) *171, 195*
Good Luck *35*
Good Morning *67*
Good Night *67*
Goose *154, 182*
Goose in the Pond *31*
Goose Tracks *30*
Goose Tracks Variation *30*
Gothic Window Border *225*
Gothic Window Corner *225*
Graduation Cap *101*
Grain Scroll *228*
Grandma's Favorite *31*
Grandmother's Basket *48*

Grandmother's Cross *17*
Grandmother's Fan *66*
Grandmother's Puzzle *31*
Granny's Choice (Adap.) *34*
Granny's Choice (Adap.) *51*
Grapes *163, 188, 190, 240*
Grapes 2 *163*
Grapes 3 *163*
Grapes of Wrath *219*
Grapes On-point *241*
Grape Basket *47*
Grape Leaf *191*
Grape Leaf 2 *192*
Grape Leaf Wreath *197*
Grape Leaves *191*
Grasshopper *148*
Graves *75*
Grecian Square *42*
Grecian Tile *172*
Greece *86*
Greek Cross *42*
Greek Key Border *225*
Greek Key Corner *225*
Greek Square *14*
Greenland *86*
Grist Mill *45*
Grogger © Debbie Sichel *112*
Grogger 2 © Debbie Sichel *112*
Grooves Border *226*
Grooves Corner *226*
Gropius *75*
Guitar *167*
Gumdrop Heart *165*
Guppy Fish *160, 184*

H

H *7, 9, 178*
h *178*
H (Foundation-Pieced Alphabet) *95*
h (Foundation-Pieced Alphabet) *94*
H is for Heart *214*
Half-Square Triangle *50, 66*
Half-Square Triangle 2 *50*
Half Checkerboard *34*
Half Sun *224*
Handbag *168*
Handkerchief Edge Border *226*
Handkerchief Edge Corner *226*
Handy Andy *30*
Hand Weave *35*
Hanukkah (Rita Denenberg) *166*
Happy Face *194*

Happy Puppy *158*
Happy Returns *67*
Harlequin *77*
Harvest Sun *61*
Hat and Pipe *166*
Haunted House *113*
Hawaiian Appliqué *164*
Hawaiian Appliqué 2 *164*
Hawaiian Appliqué 3 *164*
Hawaiian Appliqué 4 *164*
Hawaiian Appliqué 5 *164*
Hawaiian Appliqué Scroll *164*
Hawaiian Appliqué Wreath *164*
Hawaii Star *78*
Hazel Eye Compass *81*
He *67*
Heart *112, 155, 194*
Hearts & Ribbons *145*
Hearts & Sunflowers *135*
Hearts and Flowers *136*
Heart & Ribbon Meander *201*
Heart Basket *130*
Heart Blossoms *165*
Heart Dollar *166*
Heart Flag *84*
Heart Flag 2 *84*
Heart Flower *165*
Heart Flower 2 *165*
Heart Flower Bouquet *165*
Heart Lattice *218*
Heart of Leaves *165*
Heart of My Hearts (Rita Denenberg) *161*
Heart Ring *165, 206, 207*
Heart Ring 2 *206*
Heart Scrolls *166*
Heart Stars *206*
Heart Tulip Ring *206*
Heart with Candybox Ruffle *165*
Heart Wreath *212*
Heart Wreath 2 *212*
Heart Wreath 3 *212*
Heart Wreath 4 *212*
Heart Wreath 5 *212*
Heart Wreath 6 *212*
Heidi *141*
Hemlock *82*
Hen *154, 155*
Hen and Chicks *142*
Hen with Chicks Silhouette *193*
Hexagonal *29*
Hex Sign *139, 188, 225*
Hey © Debbie Sichel *92*
Hickory Wreath *197*

High Flying Squares *72*
Hither & Yon *32*
Hollow Cube *51*
Holly *152, 192*
Holly Border *152*
Honeymoon Cottage *69*
Honeysuckle *106*
Honey Locust *191*
Hong Kong *86*
Hopatcong Star *72*
Horn *152*
Horn of Plenty *137*
Horse *64, 97, 142, 155*
Horse Silhouette *193*
Hot Air Balloon *174*
Hot Latte *67*
Hourglass 1 *40*
Hourglass Puzzle *77*
Hour Glass *12, 32*
House *194*
Housefly *148*
House Beneath the Bridge *110*
House on the Hill *47*
House with Fence *113*
House with Porches *113*
Hovering Hawks *32*
Hummingbird *49*
Humpty Dumpty *151*
Hungary *86*
Hungry Cat Silhouette *149, 193*

I

I *7, 9, 178*
i *178*
I (Foundation-Pieced Alphabet) *95*
i (Foundation-Pieced Alphabet) *94*
i acute (Foundation-Pieced Alphabet) *96*
i circumflex (Foundation-Pieced Alphabet) *96*
i grave (Foundation-Pieced Alphabet) *96*
I is for Ice Cream *214*
i umlaut (Foundation-Pieced Alphabet) *96*
I Wish You Well *24*
Iceland *86*
Ice Cream Cone *194*
Ice Skates (Rita Denenberg) *171*
Ice Skate (Rita Denenberg) *195*
ickets and Points Corner *228*
Illusion *76*
Improved Four Patch *17, 51*
Improved Nine Patch *17*
India *86*
Indiana Puzzle *24, 43*

Indian Hatchets 15, 50
Indian Hatchets 2 50
Indian Hatchets Album Block 6
Indonesia 86
Information Please (Rita Denenberg) 150
Interlaced Logs 71
Interlocking Lines 203
Interlocking Rings 173, 202, 203
Interlocking Rings (border) 173, 203
Interlocking Rings Wreath 211
Interlocking Squares 173, 202
Interlocking Squares (border) 173, 203
Interwoven Square 202
Intertwined Border 224
Intertwined Corner 224
Interwoven Square 202
Iota (Greek Alphabet) 90
iota (Greek Alphabet) 90
Ireland 86
Iris 104, 106
Irish Logs 71
Iris - on point (Rita Denenberg) 161
Iris - vertical (Rita Denenberg) 161
Iris Leaves 105
Iron Gate 134
Islamic Tile 172
Israel 86
Italy 86
Ivy 115

J

J 7, 9, 178
j 178
J (Foundation-Pieced Alphabet) 95
j (Foundation-Pieced Alphabet) 94
J is for Jack-o'-Lantern 214
Jack's House 47
Jack-in-the-Box 174
Jack-O-Lantern 111
Jack in the Box 123
Jack O'Lantern (Rita Denenberg) 167
Jack of Diamonds 76
James 142
Jan's Fan 63
Jan's Star 73
January Autograph 58
Japan 86
Japanese Bamboo 133
Jelly Bean Fish 159, 184
Jelly Donut 55
Jewel 25
Jewel Star 44
Jock (Scottie) 157

Johnnie-Round-the-Corner 37
Jonquil 185
Jordan 86
Joseph's Coat 41, 45
July Autograph 58
Jumping Dog 157
Jumping Dog Silhouette 194
June Autograph 58
Jungle Flower 74
Jungle Star 77
Jupiter 70, 77

K

K 7, 9, 179
k 179
K (Foundation-Pieced Alphabet) 95
k (Foundation-Pieced Alphabet) 94
K is for Kite 214
Kaf © Debbie Sichel 92
Kaf Sofeet © Debbie Sichel 92
Kaleidoscope 26, 39, 67, 70
Kaleidoscope 2 26
Kaleidoscope Rotated 70
Kaleidoscope Variation 39
Kansas Beauty 137
Kansas Beauty On-Point 138
Kansas City 69
Kansas Star 41
Kansas Troubles 33
Kappa (Greek Alphabet) 90
kappa (Greek Alphabet) 90
Katherine 141
Kentucky Flowerpot 137
Kenya 86
Keyboard 175
Keyboard Border 226
Key Lime Pie 78
Key West 39, 217
Kikombe cha Umoja (Unity Cup) 166
King's Chain 31
King's Crown 17, 31
Kirsten's Star 78
Kissing Birds 142, 181
Kissing Birds Silhouette 193
Kitten 149
Kiwi 163
Klondike Star 52
Knotted Wave 210
Kuwait 86

L

L 7, 9, 179
l 179
L (Foundation-Pieced Alphabet) 95
l (Foundation-Pieced Alphabet) 94
L is for Leaf 214
Lacewing 148
Lacework Pot 144
Lace Shoe 169
Lace Shoe Too 170
Lacy Lattice Work 71
Ladies' Aid Block 33
Ladybug 148
Lady (Cocker Spaniel) 157
Lady of the Lake 14, 30
Lady of the Lake Flag 84
Lamda (Greek Alphabet) 91
lamda (Greek Alphabet) 91
Lamed © Debbie Sichel 93
Lantern 48
Large Center Log Cabin 116
Large Diamond Grid 210
Large Garden Urn 144
Large Tulip 139, 162
Lattice Square 33
Laurel & Lyre 216
Laurel Leaves 192
Layered Basket 99
Leaf 114, 194
Leafstem 1 105
Leafstem 2 105
Leaf Album Block 6
Leaf Cable 208
Leaf Fan 63
Leaf Meander 201
Leaf Medallion 134
Leaf Ring 208
Leaf Ring 2 208
Leaf Scroll 228
Leaf Sprig 192
Leaf Square 208
Leaf Wreath 207
Leaf Wreath with 4 Points 207
Leaf Wreath with 5 Points 207
Leaf Wreath with 6 Points 207
Leap Frog 37
Leatherwork Shoe 170
Leaves 105, 207
Leaves 2 208
Leaves and Hearts 207
Left and Right 25
Lemon 163

LeMoyne Frayed Chain *13*
LeMoyne Ray *77*
LeMoyne Ray Split *78*
LeMoyne Single Irish Chain *13*
LeMoyne Star *26, 66*
LeMoyne Star 2 *26*
LeMoyne Star 3 *26*
LeMoyne Star 4 *26*
LeMoyne Star Variation *27, 66*
LeMoyne Uneven Nine Patch *13*
Lena's Choice *27*
Letitia *141*
Letter H *37, 111*
Le Corbusier *75*
Libya *86*
Lifeguard Stand 1 *99*
Lifeguard Stand 2 *100*
Lightening Strips *79*
Lighthouse *69*
Lilacs (Rita Denenberg) *161*
Lilies *104, 106*
Lily *106, 186*
Lily (Rita Denenberg) *161*
Lily Basket *59*
Lily Block *65*
Lily Leaves *105*
Lily of the Valley (Rita Denenberg) *161*
Lily Pond from Ladies Art Company *138*
Lily Wreath *65*
Linton *35*
Little Bo Peep and Sheep *151*
Little Dipper *157, 190*
Little House *114*
Little Red Schoolhouse *48, 68*
Little Rock Block *52*
Lobster Claws *70*
Logo T-Shirt *81*
Log Cabin *14, 48, 68, 69, 114, 116*
Log Cabin (2) *14*
Log Cabin 2 *68*
Log Cabin Autograph *58*
Log Cabin Basket *60*
Log Cabin Boat *116*
Log Cabin Doll *67*
Log Cabin Flag *84*
Log Cabin Flag 2 *84*
Log Cabin Flag 3 *84*
Log Cabin House *116*
Log Cabin Pine *116*
Log Cabin Tree *82*
Lollipop Flowers *134*
London Roads *42*
Lone Star *38*

Lone Star 2 *38*
Long Handled Basket *130*
Long Vine 1 *190*
Long Vine 2 *190*
Looped Rings *202*
Looped Ring Wreath *212*
Lost Children *49*
Lost Ship Pattern *36*
Lotus Block *44*
Louvre Fan *63*
Love in a Mist *26, 38*
Love in a Mist 2 *38*
Lowey *75*
Lu's Star *73*
Lu's Star Variation *73*
Lucky Clover *33*
Lucky Star *44*
Luxembourg *86*
Lyre Scroll *228*

M

M *7, 9, 179*
m *179*
M (Foundation-Pieced Alphabet) *95*
m (Foundation-Pieced Alphabet) *94*
M is for Moon *214*
Magic Circle *36*
Magnifying Glass *175*
Maine Coon Cat *149*
Maine Lobster *64*
Malaysia *86*
Malta *86*
Maltese Cross *39*
Man *142*
Man in the Moon *157, 190*
Man Silhouette *193*
Maple *115, 124*
Maple 2 *124*
Maple 3 *124*
Maple 4 *124*
Maple 5 *124*
Maple Leaf *40, 47, 114, 192*
Maple Leaf Ring *207*
Maple Leaves *207*
Marching Triangles *116*
March Autograph *58*
Mariner's Compass *15*
Mariner's Star *15*
Mariner's Compass *16*
Martha Washington's Star *54*
Mates for Life (Rita Denenberg) *150*
May Autograph *58*

May Basket *216*
Mazao (The Crops) *166*
McMansion *113*
Meadow Flower *44, 76*
Meander Quilting *210*
Meeting Chevrons Border *238*
Meeting Chevrons Corner *238*
Meeting Double Diamonds Border *238*
Meeting Double Diamonds Corner *238*
Meeting Geese & Strips Border *237*
Meeting Geese & Strips Corner *237*
Meeting Triangles Border *238*
Meeting Triangles Corner *238*
Megan's Baskets *60*
Melon Patch *45*
Mem © Debbie Sichel *93*
Mem Sofeet © Debbie Sichel *93*
Menorah *112*
Meredith *141*
Merry Kite *35*
Mervin *141*
Metalwork *76*
Metalwork Variation *76*
Metalwork Variation 2 *76*
Mexican Blanket *79*
Mexican Rose *133, 135, 139, 187*
Mexican Rose 2 *133*
Mexican Rose 3 *135*
Mexican Rose Bush *139*
Mexican Rose Scroll *229*
Mexico *86*
Me (Rita Denenberg) *176*
Millwheel *24*
Mill and Stars *35*
Milwaukee *69*
Mishumaa (7 Candles) and Kinara (Candle
        Holder) *166*
Mississippi *41*
Missouri Puzzle *31*
Modern Milky Way *70*
Mollie's Choice *41*
Monday Autograph *58*
Monkey *98*
Monkey Overboard Compass *80*
Monkey Wrench *15, 17*
Moon *191, 194*
Moonlight *191*
Moonlight 2 *191*
Moon N Stars *191*
Moorish Design *194*
Moorish Tile *172*
More Diamonds & Strips Border *238*
More Diamonds & Strips Corner *238*

Morning Glory 106
Morning Star 53
Morning Star 2 39
Morning Star 3 39
Morning Star 4 39
Mosaic 17, 172
Mosaic, No.18 (2) 11
Mosaic, No. 1 10
Mosaic, No. 10 10
Mosaic, No. 10 (2) 11
Mosaic, No. 11 11
Mosaic, No. 13 11
Mosaic, No. 13 (2) 11
Mosaic, No. 15 11
Mosaic, No. 17 11
Mosaic, No. 18 11
Mosaic, No. 19 11
Mosaic, No. 19 (2) 11
Mosaic, No. 19 Variation 11
Mosaic, No. 1 (2) 10
Mosaic, No. 2 10
Mosaic, No. 20 11
Mosaic, No. 21 11
Mosaic, No. 21 (2) 11
Mosaic, No. 22 11
Mosaic, No. 2 (2) 10
Mosaic, No. 3 10
Mosaic, No. 3 (2) 10
Mosaic, No. 4 10
Mosaic, No. 4 (2) 10
Mosaic, No. 5 10
Mosaic, No. 5 (2) 10
Mosaic, No. 6 (6) 10
Mosaic #19 53
Mosaic #3 51
Motel 99
Moth 133, 183
Mother's Day Basket 216
Mother's Dream 17
Mouse 98
Mouse (EQ) Head 109
Mouse and Pad 175
Muhindi (Corn) 166
Mulberry Bush 82
Mule Shoe TX 72
Mum 104
Mushrooms 108
Musical Note 1 168
Musical Note 2 168
Musical Note 3 168
Musical Signs (Rita Denenberg) 168
Mu (Greek Alphabet) 91
mu (Greek Alphabet) 91

N

N 7, 9, 179
n 179
N (Foundation-Pieced Alphabet) 95
n (Foundation-Pieced Alphabet) 94
N is for Needle 214
n tilde (Foundation-Pieced Alphabet) 96
Navajo 36
Nebraska Tulips 138
Needle & Thread (Rita Denenberg) 175
Nest with Eggs 155
Netherlands Antilles 86
Nevada Star 78
New Album 17, 51
New Album Variation 6
New Hour Glass 35
New Star 36
New Year's Party Hat 167
New York Compass 117
New York Nightime 117
New York Sunburst 117
New Zealand 87
Nigeria 87
Nine 8, 10
Nine-Patch 2 Variation 41
Nine-patch Baskets 60
Nine-Patch Variation 41
Nine by Six 29
Nine Degree Wedge 74
Nine Hearts 206
Nine Patch 12, 14, 40, 50, 222
Nine Patch Album Block 6
Nine Patch Art Square 17
Nine Patch Chain 13
Nine Patch Star 31, 43
Nine Patch Star Variation 31
Noel (Rita Denenberg) 154
Non-pc Computer 176
Nonsuch 37
Northern Lights Compass 80
North Baltimore Fan 63
North Carolina Tulip 138, 186
North Carolina Tulip Cross 135
North Star 16
Norway 87
Nose-Gay 44
Nosegay Quilt from McKim Studios 137
Nosegay Swag Border 234
Nosegay Wreath 145
November Autograph 58

My Hearts of Hearts (Rita Denenberg) 166

Now Showing 218
No Tie Shirt 81
Nun © Debbie Sichel 93
Nun Sofeet © Debbie Sichel 93
Nutcracker 153
Nu (Greek Alphabet) 91
nu (Greek Alphabet) 91

O

O 7, 9, 179
o 179
O (Foundation-Pieced Alphabet) 95
o (Foundation-Pieced Alphabet) 94
o acute (Foundation-Pieced Alphabet) 96
o circumflex (Foundation-Pieced Alphabet) 96
o grave (Foundation-Pieced Alphabet) 96
O is for Orange 214
o slash (Foundation-Pieced Alphabet) 96
o tilde (Foundation-Pieced Alphabet) 96
o umlaut (Foundation-Pieced Alphabet) 96
Oak and Acorn Wreath 145
Oak and Acorn Wreath 2 145
Oak Leaf 114, 192
Oak Leaf & Reel 134
Oak Leaf 2 192
Oak Leaf 3 192
Oak Leaf and Acorn 135
Oak Leaf and Acorn 2 135
Oak Leaf and Hearts Reel 207
Oak Leaf and Reel 207
Oak Leaf Wreath 134, 197
Oak Leaf Wreath 2 134
Oak Leaf Wreath 3 134
Oak Leaves 133
Oak Leaves and Berries 207
Oak Leaves and Circles 208
Oak Leaves and Nuts 208
Oak Leaves and Reel 208
Octagon 26
Octagon Star 26
October Autograph 58
Odds and Ends 25
Odd Fellows Chain 54
Odd Fellows Chain Variation 54
Odd Scraps Patchwork 31
Off-Center 3 Log Cabin 115
Off-Center 4 Log Cabin 115
Off-Center 5 Log Cabin 116
Off-Center 6 Log Cabin 116
Off-Center 7 Log Cabin 116
Off-Center 8 Log Cabin 116
Off-Center 9 Log Cabin 116

Off-Center Log Cabin *116*
Off-side Circles *203*
Ohio Feathered Star *28*
Ohio Star *14*
Ohio Star Variation *27*
Ohio Tulips *137*
Old-Fashioned Tulip *187*
Old Country Church *48*
Old German Design *139, 187*
Old Maid's Puzzle *14, 32*
Old Maid's Ramble *37*
Old Oak *83*
Old Rose of Sharon from Canada *140, 186*
Old Snowflake *43, 76*
Old Tulips *140*
Old Two-Story *69*
Omega (Greek Alphabet) *92*
omega (Greek Alphabet) *92*
Omicron (Greek Alphabet) *91*
omicron (Greek Alphabet) *91*
On-point Basket *98*
On-point Basket 2 *98*
On-point Basket 3 *98*
On-point Basket 4 *99*
On-Point Basket with Ribbon *130*
On-point Flag *109*
On-point Flag 2 *109*
On-Point Heart *112*
On-Point Heart 2 *112*
On-Point Heart 3 *112*
On-Point Heart 4 *112*
On-Point Heart 5 *112*
On-point Layered Basket *99*
On-point Layered Basket 2 *99*
On-Point Simple Basket *130*
On-Point Tote Basket *130*
One *8, 9*
One Wheel with 12 Spokes *74*
On the Lookout *217*
Opening Gates *74*
Opposing Corners *56*
Optical Illusion *41*
Orange *108, 163, 188*
Orange Blossom *216*
Orange Peel *45, 224*
Orange Peel Border *223*
Orange Peel Corner *223*
Orange Peel Variation *45*
Orchid *106, 185*
Oriental Knot Border *225*
Oriental Knot Corner *225*
Oriental Short Hair *149*
Origami *74*

Origami Star *29*
Ornaments *153*
Ornaments with Holly *152*
Ornament with Star *152*
Ornate Star *43*
Our House (Rita Denenberg) *150*
Our Vase (Rita Denenberg) *150*
Our Wedding (Rita Denenberg) *150*
Overall Bill *143, 196*
Overlapped Snowflake Border *225*
Overlapped Snowflake Corner *225*
Overlapped Triangle Beauty *117*
Overlapped Triangle Beauty 2 *117*
Overlapping Boxes 1 *202*
Overlapping Boxes 2 *202*
Overlapping Boxes 3 *202*
Overlapping Fan *61*
Overlapping Hearts *216*
Over the Bridge *24*

P

P *7, 9, 179*
p *179*
P (Foundation-Pieced Alphabet) *95*
p (Foundation-Pieced Alphabet) *94*
P is for Penguin *214*
Paducah Peony *25*
Painted Pot *162*
Pakistan *87*
Palmate Leaf *191*
Palm Tree 1 *99*
Palm Tree 2 *99*
Palm Tree 3 *99*
Palm Tree Hawaiian Appliqué *164*
Palm Tree Hawaiian Appliqué 2 *164*
Panda *98*
Pandora's Present *111*
Pansy *48, 185*
Pansy (Rita Denenberg) *161*
Papa's Delight *45*
Papua New Guinea *87*
Parasauroplophus *173*
Partridge *153*
Party Hat *101*
Patches (Rita Denenberg) *175*
Patch as Patch Can *33*
Patch House *48*
Patriotic Patch *218*
Peaceful Hours *28*
Peace Dove *24*
Peace Dove (Rita Denenberg) *153*
Peach *108*

Peacock *98*
Peacocks *228*
Peacock Feathers *134, 172*
Peacock Feather Stencil *203*
Pear *108, 163, 188*
Pears *153*
Peas in Pods *189*
Pea Pod *189*
Pea Pods on Vine *156*
Peh © Debbie Sichel *93*
Penguin *63, 154*
Pennsylvania Dutch *139, 187, 188*
Pennsylvania Dutch Flower *186*
Pennsylvania Tulip *140, 188*
Pentagon Star *29*
Pentagon Star 2 *29*
Peonies *134*
Peonies and Lilacs (Rita Denenberg) *150*
Peony *64, 162, 185*
Peony (Rita Denenberg) *161*
Peony Blossoms *135*
Peony Border *226*
Peony Corner *226*
Pepper *108*
Period *180*
Perspective Grid 1 *74*
Perspective Grid 2 *74*
Peru *87*
Petals Stencil *205*
Petal Fan *63*
Petal Snowflake *216*
Petal Wreath *212*
Petal Wreath 2 *212*
Philadelphia *69*
Phillipines *87*
Phi (Greek Alphabet) *91*
phi (Greek Alphabet) *91*
Piano *168*
Pick-up Truck *101*
Pickets and Points Border *228*
Pickets and Stripes Border *228*
Pickets and Stripes Corner *228*
Picket and Posts *79*
Picket Border 1 *226*
Picket Border 10 *227*
Picket Border 11 *227*
Picket Border 12 *227*
Picket Border 13 *227*
Picket Border 14 *227*
Picket Border 15 *228*
Picket Border 16 *228*
Picket Border 17 *228*
Picket Border 2 *226*

Picket Border 3 *227*
Picket Border 4 *227*
Picket Border 5 *227*
Picket Border 6 *227*
Picket Border 7 *227*
Picket Border 8 *227*
Picket Border 9 *227*
Picket Corner 1 *226*
Picket Corner 10 *227*
Picket Corner 11 *227*
Picket Corner 12 *227*
Picket Corner 13 *227*
Picket Corner 14 *227*
Picket Corner 15 *228*
Picket Corner 16 *228*
Picket Corner 17 *228*
Picket Corner 2 *226*
Picket Corner 3 *227*
Picket Corner 4 *227*
Picket Corner 5 *227*
Picket Corner 6 *227*
Picket Corner 7 *227*
Picket Corner 8 *227*
Picket Corner 9 *227*
Picket Fence *69*
Pickle Dish - 4 Points *46*
Pickle Dish - 5 Points *46*
Pickle Dish - 7 Points *47*
Pickle Dish Border *223*
Pickle Dish Corner *223*
Picnic Basket *130*
Picnic Bouquet *65*
Pieced Bouquet *44*
Pig *63, 155*
Pinball Swirl *70*
Pincushion (Rita Denenberg) *175*
Pine *114, 125*
Pineapple *44, 108, 118*
Pineapple 10 *118*
Pineapple 11 *118*
Pineapple 2 *118*
Pineapple 3 *118*
Pineapple 4 *118*
Pineapple 5 *118*
Pineapple 6 *118*
Pineapple 7 *118*
Pineapple 8 *118*
Pineapple 9 *118*
Pineapple Album *118*
Pineapple Album 2 *119*
Pineapple Album 3 *119*
Pineapple Album 4 *119*
Pineapple Album 5 *119*

Pineapple ca. 1850 *140*
Pineapple Cross *135*
Pineapple Design *140, 187*
Pineapple Hawaiian Appliqué *164*
Pine 2 *125*
Pine 3 *125*
Pine 4 *125*
Pine 5 *125*
Pine Burr *49*
Pine Tree *47, 48, 112*
Pine Tree Quilt *47*
Pinwheel *32, 67*
Pinwheel Border *239*
Pinwheel Circle *54*
Pinwheel Flag *84*
Pinwheel Pine *82*
Pinwheel Square *30*
Pinwheel Star *28*
Pinwheel Variation *41*
Pin the Tail on the Donkey *101*
Pin Wheels *15*
Pi (Greek Alphabet) *91*
pi (Greek Alphabet) *91*
Plaid Fab *72*
Plaid Lattice *72*
Plain Double Wedding Ring *46*
Plain Double Wedding Ring Side *46*
Plain Heart *206*
Plain Shoe *169*
Plain Swag Border *234*
Plain Swag Corner *234*
Plain Wedding Ring *46*
Plaited Block Variation *25*
Plane *174*
Plane (Rita Denenberg) *174*
Plumes *135*
Plump Leaf *193*
Pocket Protecter *81*
Poinsettia *136, 153*
Poinsettia 2 *136*
Poinsettia Wreath *145*
Pointsettia Border (Rita Denenberg) *154*
Poland *87*
Polar Bear *154*
Polar Bear and Stars *154*
Pole Star *26*
Polywogs *64*
Pomegranate *140, 163, 188*
Pompeii *172*
Poppies *162*
Poppy *106*
Posey *139, 186*
Posey Wreath *205*

Postmodern Basket *59*
Potted Flowers *104*
Potted Star Flower *11*
Potted Star Flower Variation *11*
Pot of Roses *137*
Practical Orchard *40*
Prairie House *69*
Prairie Point Sun *80*
Prairie Star *37*
Prairie Star 2 *37*
Praying Mantis *148*
Premium Star *31*
Present *101*
Presents (Rita Denenberg) *154*
Presents Under the Tree *217*
Primrose *106*
Priscilla 2 Stripe *49*
Priscilla 3 Stripe *49*
Priscilla 4 Stripe *49*
Priscilla 5 Stripe *49*
Priscilla Variation *49*
Propeller *36, 72*
Proud Pine *47*
Providence Quilt Block *31, 52*
Prowling Cat Silhouette *149*
Psi (Greek Alphabet) *92*
psi (Greek Alphabet) *92*
Puffin *98*
Pumpkin *111, 167*
Pumpkin Seeds *203*
Pumpkin Seeds 2 *203*
Pumpkin Seeds 3 *203*
Pup *64*
Puppy *151*
Purple Coneflower *53*
Purple Petals *216*
Purse Backpack *169*
Purse with Bamboo Handle *168*
Purse with Beaded Handle *169*
Purse with Bow Handle *168*
Purse with Flower *169*
Purse with Handle *169*
Puss in the Corner *66*
Puzzle Ball *70*
Puzzle Patch *173*

Q

Q *7, 9, 179*
q *179*
Q (Foundation-Pieced Alphabet) *95*
q (Foundation-Pieced Alphabet) *94*
Q is for Queen *214*

Qatar 87
Qof © Debbie Sichel 93
Quarter-Square Triangles 66
Quarter 3 Log Cabin 115
Quarter 4 Log Cabin 115
Quarter 5 Log Cabin 115
Quarter 6 Log Cabin 115
Quarter 7 Log Cabin 115
Quarter 8 Log Cabin 115
Quarter 9 Log Cabin 115
Quarter Box-in-Box 122
Quarter Cabin 116
Quarter Cross 122
Quarter Crossing Points 122
Quarter Diagonal Triangles 122
Quarter Diamond in Square 122
Quarter Emerald City 122
Quarter Geese Block 122
Quarter Geese Block 2 122
Quarter Leaf 122
Quarter Log Cabin 110
Quarter Log Cabin 2 110
Quarter Log Cabin 3 111
Quarter Log Cabin 4 111
Quarter Log Cabin 5 111
Quarter Log Cabin 6 111
Quarter Rose 122
Quarter Rose Blooming 122
Quarter Star Flower 122
Quarter Star in a Star 122
Quarter Star with Triangles 122
Quarter Stripe with Diamond 122
Quarter T's 122
Quarter Wedding Ring 14
Quarter Windmill 122
Quarter Woven Star 122
Quarter Woven Star 2 122
Queen Angel Fish 64

R

R 7, 9, 179
r 179
R (Foundation-Pieced Alphabet) 95
r (Foundation-Pieced Alphabet) 94
R is for Robot 214
Rabbit 64, 98, 158
Rabbit Head 109
Race Car 100
Radiant Beauty 117
Radiant Star 28
Radiating Petals 205
Radical Rose 140

Radish 156, 189
Radishes 108
Rag Doll 123
Rail Fence 14, 110
Rail Fence 2 110
Rail Fence 3 110
Rail Fence Flag 84
Rail Fence Quilt 65
Rainbow 194
Rainbow Border 223
Rainbow Corner 223
Rainbow Fan 61
Rainbow Logs 71
Rainbow Rosie Fish 159, 184
Rainbow Star 38
Rainbow Star 2 38
Rainbow Steps 79
Raleigh 45
Random Stripes 79
Random Stripes 2 79
Raspberries 163
Raspberry Cream 78
Rectangular Center Log Cabin 116
Red and White Cross 33
Red Barn 48
Red Cross 31
Red Fox 64
Red Maple 83
Red Oak 114
Red Tulip 105
Reeds 184
Reel 146
Reindeer 64, 152
Relaxed Corner (In) 189
Relaxed Corner (In) with Flowers 240
Relaxed Corner (In) with Leaves 190
Relaxed Corner (In) with Pomegranates 240
Relaxed Corner (Out) 189
Relaxed Corner (Out) with Bird and Berries 241
Relaxed Corner (Out) with Leaves 190
Relaxed Grape Vine 241
Relaxed Vine 189, 239
Relaxed Vine Corner (In) 239
Relaxed Vine Corner (In) with Leaves 240
Relaxed Vine Corner (Out) 239, 241
Relaxed Vine Corner (Out) with Leaves 240
Relaxed Vine with Bird and Berries 241
Relaxed Vine with Flowers 240
Relaxed Vine with Grapes 240
Relaxed Vine with Grapes and Leaves 240
Relaxed Vine with Honeysuckle 241
Relaxed Vine with Leaves 190, 240
Relaxed Vine with Pomegranates 240

Resh © Debbie Sichel 93
Rhinoceros 98
Rhode Island 42
Rhode Island Star 78
Rho (Greek Alphabet) 91
rho (Greek Alphabet) 91
Rhubarb Pie 78
Ribbed Vase 144
Ribbon 150, 152
Ribbons 25
Ribbons and Hearts 207
Ribbons and Hearts 2 207
Ribbons and Stars 208
Ribbon Autograph 58
Ribbon Border 25
Ribbon Frame 208
Ribbon Frame 2 208
Ribbon Meander 200
Ribbon Medallion 145
Ribbon Quilt 43
Ribbon Vine 209
Ribbon with Three Bows 208
Ribbon Wreath 209
Ribbon Wreath 2 209
Rick-Rack Basket 59
Rick-Rack Star 27
Rick Rack Beauty 117
Rick Rack Beauty 2 117
Rick Rack Medallion 55
Right and Left 17, 25, 51
Rings and Squares 202
Rings and Squares 2 202
Ring Around the Posey 206
Ring Chain (corner) 173, 203
Ring of Hearts 207
Ring Those Bells (Rita Denenberg) 153
Rising Star 16, 53
Rising Sun 16, 61
Rising Waves 216
Rita 141
Road to California 12, 13, 41
Road to California Variation 13
Road to Fortune 44
Road to Oklahoma 12, 15
Robin on Branch 155, 182
Robot 1 175
Robot 2 175
Roche 75
Rocket 174, 175
Rockingham's Beauty 49
Rockingham's Beauty Variation 49
Rocking Horse 123, 152
Rocky Fish 159, 184

Rocky Road to California *13*
Rocky Road to Kansas *49*
Roller Blade (Rita Denenberg) *171*
Roller Skate (Rita Denenberg) *195*
Rolling Crosses *70*
Rolling Feathered Star *28*
Rolling Hearts *206*
Rolling Hearts 2 *206*
Rolling Hearts 3 *206*
Rolling Hearts 4 *206*
Rolling Plate *53*
Rolling Rock *77*
Rolling Squares *41*
Rolling Star *26, 27, 38*
Rolling Star 2 *38*
Rolling Star 3 *38*
Rolling Stone *41*
Rolling Wheel Beauty *118*
Roman Cross *36*
Roman Stripe *79*
Roman Villa *172*
Rooster *142, 155, 181*
Rooster Silhouette *193*
Rooster Weathervane *139, 188*
Rose *48, 65, 104, 139, 161, 187*
Rosebud *35, 65, 162*
Rosebuds *141*
Rosebud Wreath *211*
Roses and Butterfly *163*
Rose & Buds *138*
Rose (Rita Denenberg) *161*
Rose and Buds *162, 186*
Rose and Buds Quatrefoil *197*
Rose and Tulip from Grandma Dexter *145*
Rose Appliqué *140, 186*
Rose Border (Rita Denenberg) *161*
Rose Bouquet *186*
Rose Bouquet with Stars *140*
Rose Bud *186*
Rose Covered Shoe *170*
Rose from New Jersey Sampler *140*
Rose in Bloom *140*
Rose in Bud *136*
Rose of LeMoyne *140, 186*
Rose of Sharon *135, 137, 140, 141, 185*
Rose of Sharon from McKim Studios *140*
Rose of Sharon from Tennessee *136*
Rose of Sharon On-Point *138*
Rose of Sharon Wreath *141*
Rose Ring *141*
Rose Sprigs *197*
Rose Stencil *205*
Rose Tree *140, 186*

Rose Window *70, 206*
Rose with Bud *186*
Rose with Buds *133*
Rose Wreath *141, 205*
Rose Wreath 2 *141*
Rose Wreath from New Jersey Sampler *145*
Rose Wreath in a Diamond *215*
Rotary Cutter (Rita Denenberg) *175*
Rotary Ribbon *71*
Rotate Me *76*
Rotate Surprise *215*
Rotating Stars *218*
Round Basket *99, 130*
Round Cabin *71*
Round Table *54*
Row of Poplars *114*
Royal Diamonds *26*
Roycroft *75*
Rubber Ducky *123*
Rudolph the Red-Nosed Reindeer *153*
Rudy Fish *159, 183*
Russian Federation *87*

S

S *7, 9, 179*
s *179*
S (Foundation-Pieced Alphabet) *95*
s (Foundation-Pieced Alphabet) *94*
S is for Snowflake *214*
Sadie (Lab) *157*
Sailboat *109, 174*
Sailboat 2 *109, 174*
Sailboat 3 *109, 174*
Sailboat 4 *109*
Sailboat Quilt *47*
Sailor's Delight *217*
Saltbox *69*
Sam *143, 196*
Samech © Debbie Sichel *93*
Sammy the Spastic Wonder Dog *158*
Sand Castle *100*
Sand Dollar *70*
Sand Dune 1 *99*
Sand Dune 2 *99*
Santa *111, 152*
Santa Fe Block *36*
Sara's Star *73*
Sara's Star Variation *73*
Sarah's Choice *53*
Sarah's Favorite *34*
Sashed Medallion *55*
Sassafras *192*

Savannah Beautiful Star *29*
Savannah Star *72*
Sawtooth 16 Patch *53*
Sawtooth Border *235*
Sawtooth Corner *236*
Sawtooth Fan *61*
Sawtooth Medallion *55*
Sawtooth Star *53*
Sawtooth Wreath *212*
Saw Tooth *42*
Saxophone *167*
Saxophone with Notes *167*
Sax (Rita Denenberg) *167*
Scaley Fish *160, 184*
Scalloped Swag Border *234*
Scalloped Swag with Large Ribbons *234*
Scalloped Swag with Small Ribbons *234*
Scallops *211*
Scattered Blossoms *197*
Scattered Leaves *216*
Scattered Roses *197*
Schoolhouse *69*
School Bus *100*
School Girl's Puzzle *33*
School Girl's Puzzle (2) *33*
Schooner *109*
Scilla *186*
Scissors (Rita Denenberg) *175*
Scotland *87*
Scrappy Stripper *71*
Scrap Basket *59*
Scrap Blossoms *73*
Scrap Chevrons *79*
Scrap Sparkler *77*
Scrap Violet *76*
Scroll with Thorns and Diamonds *228*
Scroll with Thorns and Diamonds 2 *229*
Secret Star *77*
Sedan *100*
Sedona's Sun *81*
Sedona Star *72*
Seeds & Waves *204*
Seed Packet Row Marker *156*
Seed Packet Row Marker 2 *156*
Seminole Stripes Border *239*
Semi Truck *101*
Senegal *87*
September Autograph *58*
September Flower *78*
Setting Sun *44*
Seven *8, 10*
Seven Lines *211*
Sewing Machine *68, 175*

Shadow Arc Beauty *117*
Shadow Star *72*
Shady Window *215*
Shagbark Hickory *191*
Shamrocks *162, 166*
Sharky Fish *160, 184*
Sharon's Love *135*
She *67*
Sheep *158*
She and He (Judy Vigiletti) *68*
Shining Bright *74*
Shin © Debbie Sichel *93*
Shirt & Sweater *81*
Shirt and Sweater *81*
Shoe with Bow *169*
Shoe with Buckle *170*
Shoe with Flower *169*
Shoe with Flower Buttons *170*
Shoe with Strap *169*
Shooting Star *27*
Shooting Stars *28*
Shoo Fly *14, 40, 50*
Sigma (Greek Alphabet) *91*
sigma (Greek Alphabet) *91*
Silk Rainbow *63*
Silver and Gold *26*
Silver Maple *44, 114, 191*
Simple Bargello *79*
Simple Basket *130*
Simple Bird *143*
Simple Ribbon *208*
Simple Ribbon 2 *208*
Simple Ribbon 3 *208*
Simple Star Wreath *211*
Simple Tote *169*
Simple Urn *144*
Simple Vase *144*
Simple Wreath *212*
Singapore *87*
Single Celtic Heart *165*
Single Flower *136, 186*
Single Irish Chain *13*
Single Leaf Swag Border *234*
Single Wave *210*
Sister's Choice *31*
Sitting Cat Silhouette *149, 193*
Sitting Sue *196*
Six *8, 10*
Six-Pointed Star *29*
Sixteen Patch *32, 222*
Sixteen Points *32*
Six Blades *54*
Six Heart Ring *206*

Six Heart Ring 2 *206*
Six Lines *211*
Skipper Fish *159, 183*
Slanting Stripes & Strips Border *237*
Slanting Stripes & Strips Corner *237*
Slashed Album *25*
Sleepy Cat *149*
Sleep Tight *217*
Sleigh *152*
Slovenia *87*
Small Dahlia *56*
Small Leaf Wreath with 4 Points *207*
Small Pine *125*
Small Ribbon Swag Border *234*
Small Tulip *187*
Smiling Cartoon Cat *149*
Smoke *191*
Smoochie Fish *159, 184*
Snail's Trail *17*
Snake *109*
Snow-covered Cabin *191*
Snow-covered Tree *190*
Snow-topped Tree *125*
Snowball *40, 45*
Snowball Variation *40*
Snowdrop *105*
Snowflake *153*
Snowflake 1 *71*
Snowflake 2 *71*
Snowflake 3 *71*
Snowflake 4 *71*
Snowflake Feathered Star *28*
Snowman *152*
Snowshoe Cat *149*
Snowy Day *217*
Snowy Pine *82*
Soccer Ball *170*
Sophia *142*
Southern Star *16*
Southwestern House *113*
South Africa *87*
South Korea *87*
South Pole Star *80*
Spaceman Doll *174*
Spades on Spades *134*
Spiderweb Maltese 2 *39*
Spiderweb Maltese 3 *39*
Spiderweb Maltese 4 *39*
Spiderweb Star *27*
Spiderweb Star 2 *27*
Spikey Flower Swag Border *234*
Spike Fish *160, 184*
Spinning Blades *74*

Spinning Snowflake *218*
Spinning Stars Variation *35, 51*
Spiral Roses *218*
Split 12 Point Star *52*
Split Bars *79*
Split Center Log Cabin *116*
Split Eight Blades *55*
Split Four Blades *55*
Split Four Patch Circle *55*
Split Level House *113*
Split Six Blades *55*
Split Sunflower Border *224*
Split Sunflower Corner *224*
Split Ten Blades *55*
Spool *14*
Spools *33*
Spool 2 *51*
Spool of Thread *175*
Spool of Thread (Rita Denenberg) *175*
Sports Car *100*
Spring Beauty *45*
Spring Flowers *215*
Spring Flowers Border *226*
Spring Flowers Corner *226*
Spring Tulips *138*
Sprouting Orchids *206*
Spruce *125*
Spruce 2 *125*
Spruce 3 *125*
Square-in-Diamond *55*
Square-in-Square Star *28*
Square and a Half *30, 52*
Square Dance *67*
Square in a Square *16*
Squash *108*
Squirrel *158*
St. Louis *69*
St. Louis Star *30*
St. Louis Star Variation *26*
Staccato Border *225*
Staccato Corner *225*
Staggered Hearts *206*
Stained-Glass Window *215*
Stained Glass 6 Twist *120*
Stained Glass 7 Twist *120*
Stained Glass American Chain *120*
Stained Glass Basket *121*
Stained Glass Blunt Square on Point *120*
Stained Glass Candle *121*
Stained Glass Circle *120*
Stained Glass Cracker *119*
Stained Glass Cracker 2 *120*
Stained Glass Diamond in Square *119*

Stained Glass Diamond in Square 2 *119*
Stained Glass Diamond in Square 3 *119*
Stained Glass Diamond in Square 4 *119*
Stained Glass Diamond in Square 5 *119*
Stained Glass Diamond in Square 6 *120*
Stained Glass Diamond in Square 7 *120*
Stained Glass Diamond with Borders *119*
Stained Glass Flag *121*
Stained Glass Flower *121*
Stained Glass H *119*
Stained Glass Heart *121*
Stained Glass Heart 2 *121*
Stained Glass House *121*
Stained Glass House 2 *121*
Stained Glass Log Cabin *120*
Stained Glass Log Cabin 2 *120*
Stained Glass Log Cabin 3 *120*
Stained Glass Log Cabin 4 *120*
Stained Glass Log Cabin 5 *120*
Stained Glass Log Cabin 6 *121*
Stained Glass Log Cabin Triangle *120*
Stained Glass Log Cabin Variation *120*
Stained Glass Log Cabin Variation 2 *120*
Stained Glass Pineapple 1 *120*
Stained Glass Pineapple 2 *120*
Stained Glass Pineapple 3 *120*
Stained Glass Pineapple 4 *120*
Stained Glass Pineapple 5 *120*
Stained Glass Pineapple 6 *120*
Stained Glass Pine Tree 1 *121*
Stained Glass Pine Tree 2 *121*
Stained Glass Pine Tree 3 *121*
Stained Glass Pine Tree 4 *121*
Stained Glass Sailboat *121*
Stained Glass Stripes *121*
Stained Glass Stripes 2 *121*
Stained Glass Surrounded Square *120*
Stained Glass Tree 1 *121*
Stained Glass Tree 2 *121*
Stained Glass Tree 3 *121*
Stained Glass Uneven Log Cabin *120*
Standing Basket *59*
Standing Bird 2 *181*
Standing Bird 3 *181*
Standing Cat Silhouette *149*
Star *153, 191, 194, 209*
Star-in-Square *209*
Star-in-Star *30*
Starburst *209*
Starburst Wreath *211*
Starched Shirt *81*
Starfish *160*
Starflower *71*

Starlight *27*
Starlight Variation *27*
Starry Night *27*
Starry Path *44*
Stars *210*
Starshine Beauty *117*
Stars & Beams *209*
Stars & Beams Variation *73*
Stars and Arcs *30*
Stars and Hearts Forever *165*
Stars and Lilies *27*
Stars and Stripes *218*
Star & Pinwheels *53*
Star 2 *209*
Star and Chains *36*
Star and Crescent *29*
Star and Cubes *34*
Star Dahlia *78*
Star Flower *71*
Star Flowers *27*
Star Group *190*
Star of Bethlehem *27, 28, 29, 38*
Star of Bethlehem 2 *38*
Star of David (Debbie Sichel) *68*
Star of David 2 (Debbie Sichel) *68*
Star of David 3 (Debbie Sichel) *68*
Star of David 4 (Debbie Sichel) *68*
Star of North Carolina *35*
Star of North Carolina Variation *35*
Star of the East *26, 29, 39*
Star of the West *29*
Star Puzzle *54*
Star Swirl *77, 209*
Star Variation *26, 43, 52*
Star Wheel *15*
Star within Stars *218*
Star within Sun *80*
Star Wreath *209*
Station Wagon *101*
Steeplechase *24*
Stegosaurus *173*
Stellie *41*
Stem *105*
Stem and Leaves *105*
Stencil Leaf *191*
Stencil Leaf Wreath *197*
Stencil Leaf 2 *193*
Stencil Tulips *139, 162*
Steps to the Altar *37*
Stickley *75*
Stocking *152*
Stork and Baby *150*
Stork and Bundle of Joy *102*

Storm at Sea *36, 44, 55*
Storm Signal *33*
Strappy Shoe *170*
Strawberries *108, 163*
Strawberry *156, 189*
String Star *72, 76*
Striped Bag *168*
Striped Bag 2 *169*
Striped Bag 3 *169*
Striped Basket *98*
Striped Big & Little *82*
Striped Bowl on Cloth *99*
Striped Curved-handle Basket *98*
Striped Floral *215*
Striped Grooves Border *226*
Striped Grooves Corner *226*
Striped Lattice Work *72*
Striped Squares *79*
Striped Vase *105, 144*
Stripe and Strips Border *236*
Stripe and Strips Border 2 *236*
Stripe and Strips Border 3 *236*
Stripe and Strips Corner *236*
Stripe and Strips Corner 2 *236*
Stripe and Strips Corner 3 *236*
Stripe Border 1 *232*
Stripe Border 10 *233*
Stripe Border 11 *233*
Stripe Border 12 *233*
Stripe Border 13 *233*
Stripe Border 14 *233*
Stripe Border 2 *232*
Stripe Border 3 *232*
Stripe Border 4 *232*
Stripe Border 5 *233*
Stripe Border 6 *233*
Stripe Border 7 *233*
Stripe Border 8 *233*
Stripe Border 9 *233*
Stripe Corner 1 *232*
Stripe Corner 10 *233*
Stripe Corner 11 *233*
Stripe Corner 12 *233*
Stripe Corner 13 *233*
Stripe Corner 14 *233*
Stripe Corner 2 *232*
Stripe Corner 3 *232*
Stripe Corner 4 *232*
Stripe Corner 5 *233*
Stripe Corner 6 *233*
Stripe Corner 7 *233*
Stripe Corner 8 *233*
Stripe Corner 9 *233*

Strippy Bars *79*
Strippy Block *225*
Strips and Strings Border *225*
Strips and Strings Corner *225*
Strip Circles *71*
Strip Heart *112*
Strip Heart 2 *112*
Strip Star *72*
Stuffed Shirt *81*
Sue On-point *144*
Sue Picks Tulips *143, 196*
Sue Redux *143, 196*
Sue with Balloons *144, 196*
Sue with Pocket *196*
Sugar Bowl *17, 45, 224*
Sugar Creek Basket *59*
Sugar Maple *82, 114*
Sullivan *75*
Summer Block *162*
Summer Block (quarter design) *161*
Summer Winds *41*
Sun *157, 194*
Sunbeam *53*
Sunbeam Variation *53*
Sunbonnet (Rita Denenberg) *155*
Sunbonnet Girl with Bouquet *143*
Sunbonnet Girl with Watering Can *143*
Sunbonnet Sue *143, 196*
Sunbonnet Sue as Little Boy Blue *196*
Sunbonnet Sue as Little Bo Peep *196*
Sunburst *15*
Sunburst and Mills *38*
Sunburst Beauty *117*
Sunflower *64, 185*
Sunflowers *47*
Sunflowers in a Pot *162*
Sunflower (Rita Denenberg) *161*
Sunflower Clutch *169*
Sunflower Fence *156*
Sunflower in Heart *187*
Sunflower Wreath *212*
Sunny Jim *143, 196*
Sunny Sail *217*
Sunrise *16, 109*
Sun & Shadow Basket *59*
Sun & Shadow Baskets *59*
Sun Bonnet Girl from Grandmother Clark, 1931 *196*
Sun Bonnet Girl with Bouquet *196*
Sun Circle *80*
Sun Compass 1 *80*
Sun Compass 2 *80*
Sun Compass 3 *80*

Sun Compass 4 *80*
Sun Rings *80*
Sun Rings 2 *80*
Sun Rings 3 *81*
Sun Rings 4 *81*
Sun Spin *78*
Sun Spokes *80*
Sun Spokes 2 *80*
Sun Swirl *80*
Sun Wheel 1 *80*
Sun Wheel 2 *80*
Sun Wreath *211*
Surprise *157*
Surprise Package *111*
Susannah (Variation) *17*
Suspenders *81*
SUV *101*
Swallowtail Butterfly *132, 182*
Swallowtail Butterfly 2 *133, 183*
Swamp Angel *43*
Swan *63, 98, 131, 181*
Sweden *87*
Sweetgum *114*
Sweet Dreams *217*
Sweet Gum *82, 191*
Sweet Peas *133*
Swing in the Center *43*
Swirling Petals *205*
Switzerland *87*
Sycamore Leaf *192*
Sydney (German Shepard) *157*
Sylvia *141*

T

T *7, 9, 179*
t *179*
T (Foundation-Pieced Alphabet) *95*
t (Foundation-Pieced Alphabet) *94*
T is for Telephone *214*
T Quartette *37*
T-Shirt *81*
Tabby *149*
Taiwan *87*
Tall Pine *125*
Tall Pines *124*
Tall Star *76*
Tall Tree *124*
Tangled Lines *25*
Tangled Stars *25*
Tanzania *87*
Tau (Greek Alphabet) *91*
tau (Greek Alphabet) *91*

Tav © Debbie Sichel *93*
Teague *75*
Teddy Bear *123*
Teddy Bear 1 *171*
Teddy Bear 2 *171*
Teddy Bear 3 *171*
Teddy Bear 4 *171*
Teddy Bear 5 *171*
Teddy Bear 6 *171*
Teddy Bear 7 *171*
Teddy Bear and Gift *152*
Teddy Bear with Ball *171*
Teddy Bear with Block *172*
Teddy Bear with Daisy *172*
Teddy Bear with Daisy 2 *172*
Teddy Bear with Daisy 3 *172*
Teddy Bear with Flowers *172*
Teddy Bear with Heart *171*
Teddy Bear with Honey *171*
Teddy Bear with Ice Cream *172*
Teddy Bear with Shirt *171*
Teddy Bear with Tulip (Rita Denenberg) *151*
Teddy Bear with Vest *171*
Ted E. Bear *174*
Telephone *175*
Temple Court *32*
Tent *194*
Ten Blades *54*
Terrie's in Taos *69*
Tet © Debbie Sichel *92*
Texas Flower *36*
Texas Flower Autograph *58*
Texas Ranger *49*
Texas Tears *37*
Texas Wheel *219*
Thailand *87*
Theta (Greek Alphabet) *90*
theta (Greek Alphabet) *90*
The 18th Hole (Rita Denenberg) *171, 195*
The Airplane *47*
The Arrowhead *34*
The Bahamas *84*
The Butterfly Quilt (2) *47*
The Diversion Quilt *51*
The Harvard Club *81*
The Lake Cottage *69*
The Letter X *40*
The Maestro (Rita Denenberg) *168*
The Mayflower *25, 51*
The Netherlands *86*
The Old Homestead *47*
The Palm *44*
The Priscilla *49, 51*

The Priscilla (EasyDraw) 25
The Priscilla (PatchDraw) 25
The Spool 40, 50
The Windmill 42
Thimbles 68
Thimble (Rita Denenberg) 175
Thirteen Lines 211
Thirties Blossoms 133
thorn (Foundation-Pieced Alphabet) 97
Three 8, 10
Three-Part Flower 138, 162
Three-Part Flower 2 138, 162
Three by Three 42
Three by Two 32
Three Clouds 190
Three Trees 82
Three Wheels with 12 Spokes 74
Thrifty 13
Thundercloud 157
Thursday Autograph 58
Tie Fan 2 62
Tie Fan 3 62
Tie Fan 5 62
Tie Fan 6 62
Tie Fan 7 62
Tie Fan 8 62
Tie Fan 4 62
Tiger Fish 159, 183
Tiger Lily 137
Tiger Lily (Rita Denenberg) 161
Tight Corner (In) 189
Tight Corner (In) with Circle Flower 240
Tight Corner (In) with Complex Leaves 240
Tight Corner (In) with Flower and Bud 240
Tight Corner (In) with Leaves 190
Tight Corner (Out) with Grapes 189, 240
Tight Grape Vine 190, 241
Tight Pineapple 1 119
Tight Pineapple 2 119
Tight Pineapple 3 119
Tight Pineapple 4 119
Tight Pineapple 5 119
Tight Pineapple 6 119
Tight Pineapple 7 119
Tight Vine 189, 240
Tight Vine Corner (In) 240
Tight Vine Corner (In) with Leaves 240
Tight Vine Corner (Out) 239
Tight Vine Corner (Out) with Leaves 240
Tight Vine with Circle Flower 240
Tight Vine with Complex Leaves 240
Tight Vine with Flower and Bud 240
Tight Vine with Grapes 189, 240

Tight Vine with Grapes and Leaves 189, 240
Tight Vine with Leaves 190, 240
Tiled Stars 210
Tile Floor 209
Tile Overall 210
Tilted 1 127
Tilted 2 127
Tilted 3 127
Tilted 4 127
Tilted 5 127
Tilted 6 127
Tilted 7 127
Time & Tide 41
Tiny House 110
Tiny House Too 110
Tiny Pine 125
Tomato 108, 156, 189
Topeka Rose 141
Topiary 59
Topiary Trio 82
Topiary Trio 3 82
Topiary Trio Too 82
Topsy-Turvy House 110
Tote Basket 130
Townhouses 1 113
Townhouses 2 113
Toy Barn 67
Toy Blocks 123
Toy Boat 123
Toy Brontosaurus 123
Toy Duck 174
Toy Lamb 123
Toy Rabbit 123
Toy Robot 123
Toy Rocket 123, 174
Toy Tyrannosaurus Rex 123
Tractor 174
Trading Post 77
Train Engine Wind-up 174
Tramp Art Frame Border 226
Tramp Art Frame Corner 226
Transparent Circle 55
Treble Clef 168
Treble Staff 168
Tree 112, 194
Tree Everlasting 14, 79
Tree Everlasting Border 238
Tree Everlasting Corner 238
Tree in the Forest 83
Tree in the Snow 153
Tree of Heaven 191
Tree of Life 47, 155
Tree on a Hill 83, 124

Tree with Spacer 124
Trellis 216
Trellis Vines 134
Triangles and Strips Border 236
Triangles and Strips Border 2 237
Triangles and Strips Border 3 237
Triangles and Strips Corner 237
Triangles and Strips Corner 2 237
Triangles and Strips Corner 3 237
Triangles Border 238
Triangles Corner 238
Triangle Tree 82
Triangle Tree 2 83
Triangular Border 1 235
Triangular Border 2 235
Triangular Border 3 235
Triangular Border 4 235
Triangular Border 5 235
Triangular Border 6 235
Triangular Border 7 235
Triangular Border 8 235
Triangular Border 9 235
Triangular Corner 1A 235
Triangular Corner 2 235
Triangular Corner 3 235
Triangular Corner 4 235
Triangular Corner 5 235
Triangular Corner 6A 235
Triangular Corner 6B 235
Triangular Corner 8 235
Triangular Corner 9 235
Triceratops 173
Trick or Treat Pumpkin 166
Trick or Treat (Rita Denenberg) 167
Tricycle 123, 174
Triple 3-D Zig Zag Border 239
Triple 3-D Zig Zag Corner 239
Triple Irish Chain 13
Triple Slanting Strips Border 237
Triple Slanting Strips Corner 237
Triple Stripe 17
Triple Triangles Border 237
Triple Triangles Corner 237
Triple Triangle Star 29
Tropical Bird 131, 181
True Lover's Knot 34, 45
Trumpet 167
Trumpet Vine 48
Tsadi © Debbie Sichel 93
Tsadi Sofeet © Debbie Sichel 93
Tudor Mansion 113
Tuesday Autograph 58
Tulip 65, 105, 160

Tulips *133, 160*
Tulips 2 *133*
Tulips from 1855 Album Quilt *137*
Tulips in a Tangle *197*
Tulips in Pot *137*
Tulips in Urn *137*
Tulips in Urn On-Point *138*
Tulips Scrolls *229*
Tulip and Leaves *185*
Tulip and Pomegranate *135*
Tulip and Sun *138*
Tulip Appliqué *136, 138*
Tulip Basket *11, 12*
Tulip Basket Variation *11*
Tulip Block *162*
Tulip Block 2 *162*
Tulip Bowl from North Carolina *137*
Tulip Brocade *135*
Tulip Bud *104*
Tulip Cross *135*
Tulip from North Carolina *136*
Tulip from North Carolina Quilt *136*
Tulip from North Carolina Quilt 2 *136*
Tulip Garden *138*
Tulip Hawaiian Appliqué *164*
Tulip Heads *185*
Tulip Leaves *105*
Tulip Ring *145, 197, 205*
Tulip Tree *138, 162*
Tulip Tree 2 *138*
Tulip Tree Leaves *133*
Tumbling Cube *77*
Tumbling Star *77*
Turkey *63*
Turnip *156, 189*
Turnstile *32*
Turtle *24*
Twelve Triangles *16, 51, 111*
Twenty-Five Patch *30*
Twenty-One Lines *211*
Twinkling Stars *191*
Twin Sisters *35, 51, 66*
Twin Sisters Variation *35*
Twin Star *42*
Twisted Log Cabin 1 *125*
Twisted Log Cabin 2 *125*
Twisted Log Cabin 3 *125*
Twisted Log Cabin 4 *125*
Twisted Log Cabin 5 *126*
Twisted Log Cabin 6 *126*
Twisted Log Cabin 7 *126*
Twisted Rope Border *225*
Twisted Rope Corner *225*

Twisting Feathers *204*
Twisting Feathers 2 *204*
Twist 1 *126*
Twist 10 *126*
Twist 11 *126*
Twist 12 *126*
Twist 13 *126*
Twist 14 *126*
Twist 15 *126*
Twist 16 *126*
Twist 17 *126*
Twist 18 *126*
Twist 19 *126*
Twist 2 *126*
Twist 20 *126*
Twist 21 *126*
Twist 22 *127*
Twist 23 *127*
Twist 24 *127*
Twist 25 *127*
Twist 3 *126*
Twist 4 *126*
Twist 5 *126*
Twist 6 *126*
Twist 7 *126*
Twist 8 *126*
Twist 9 *126*
Two *8, 9*
Two-Tone Boot with Laces *169*
Two-Tone Shoe *170*
Two Buds *161*
Two Buds 2 *161*
Two by Three *42*
Two by Two *32*
Two Clouds *156, 190*
Two Friends (Judy Vigiletti) *68*
Two Pines *114*
Two Tall Trees *124*
Two Turtle Doves *101*
Tyrolean Design *162*

U

U *8, 9, 179*
u *179*
U (Foundation-Pieced Alphabet) *95*
u (Foundation-Pieced Alphabet) *94*
u acute (Foundation-Pieced Alphabet) *97*
u circumflex (Foundation-Pieced Alphabet) *97*
u grave (Foundation-Pieced Alphabet) *97*
U is for Umbrella *215*
u umlaut (Foundation-Pieced Alphabet) *97*
Ucello's Shield *74*

Ukraine *87*
Umbrella Tree *83, 124*
Uncle Sam's Hourglass *52*
Under the Rainbow *114*
Uneven Cross X *66*
Uneven Nine Patch *12*
Uneven Star *77*
Union Star *29*
United Arab Emirates *87*
United Kingdom *87*
United States *83*
Upsilon (Greek Alphabet) *91*
upsilon (Greek Alphabet) *91*
Up and Down Triangles Border *238*
Up and Down Triangles Corner *238*

V

V *8, 9, 179*
v *179*
V (Foundation-Pieced Alphabet) *95*
v (Foundation-Pieced Alphabet) *94*
V Block *39*
V Block Star *39*
V is for Violin *215*
V-Lines *210*
V-Lines 2 *210*
V-Lines 3 *210*
Valentine's Hawaiian Appliqué *164*
Valentine Album *216*
Valentine Sue *143, 196*
Valentine Swag Border *234*
Valentine Wreath *145*
Van *101*
Variable Star *42, 53*
Variable Star Variation *53*
Variable Violet Star *216*
Vase *144*
Vase of Flowers *48*
Vase with Handles *144*
Vase with Mixed Bouquet *137*
Vav © Debbie Sichel *92*
Venezuela *88*
Vines at the Window *33*
Violet Nosegay *185*
Violet Star Bouquet *216*
Violin *167*
Violin (Rita Denenberg) *167*
Volleyball *171, 195*
VW Beetle *148*

W

W *8, 9, 180*
w *180*
W (Foundation-Pieced Alphabet) *95*
w (Foundation-Pieced Alphabet) *94*
W is for Watering Can *215*
W.C.T. Union *37*
Wagon Wheel *54*
Wake Up *217*
Walking Cat Silhouette *149*
Walking X *74*
Wally Fish *160, 184*
Washington's Puzzle *25*
Wasp *148*
Watering Can *144, 156*
Watermelon *140, 188*
Watermelon Slice *156, 189*
Water Lily *184*
Water Lily 2 *184*
Water Lily Pad *184*
Water Lily Pads *184*
Water Lily Pads 2 *184*
Water Pitcher *144*
Waves *100*
Waves and Fish *100*
Waving Flag *79*
Waving Grid *211*
Wavy & Straight *211*
Wavy Lines *210*
Wavy Lines 2 *210*
Wavy Lines 3 *210*
Wavy Ribbon *208*
Weathervane *18*
Weathervane Variation *18*
Wedding Bells *101*
Wedding Cake *101*
Wedding Ring - 4 Segments *46*
Wedding Ring - 5 Segments *46*
Wedding Ring - 7 Segments *46*
Wedding Ring Border *223*
Wedding Ring Corner *223*
Wednesday Autograph *58*
Welcome Home *158*
Western Spy *27*
We Grew Roses (Rita Denenberg) *161*
Wheel *203*
Wheel 2 *203*
Wheel of Chance *55*
Wheel of Fortune *36, 54*
Whirligig *44, 76*
Whirling Buds & Berries *216*
Whirling Star *33*

Whirlpool *32*
Whirlwind *15, 51*
Whirlwind Flag *84*
White Cross *34*
White Oak *114, 191*
Wide Cross X *66*
Widower's Choice *36*
Wildflower Bouquet *162*
Wildflower Ring *145*
Wildflower Swag Border *234*
Wildflower Wreath *145*
Wild Goose 2 Variation *52*
Wild Goose Chase *15, 52, 66, 79*
Wild Goose Chase Border *236*
Wild Goose Chase Corner *236*
Wild Goose Flag *83*
Wild Goose Flag 2 *83*
Wild Goose Log Cabin *116*
Wild Goose Variation *51*
Willow *83*
Windmill *32, 67, 74, 77*
Windmill 2 *77*
Windmill and Outline *35, 51*
Windmill Variation *74*
Windsurf Board *100*
Wind Blown Rose *197*
Wineglass *203*
Wineglass (Straight) *204*
Wineglass 2 *203*
Wisconsin Cabin *69*
Wise Men (Rita Denenberg) *153*
Witch *111*
Witch (Rita Denenberg) *167*
Woman *142*
Woman Silhouette *193*
Work Box *25*
Work Shirt *81*
World's Fair Puzzle *36*
World Globe *174*
World Without End Variation *50*
Woven Basket *59, 130*
Woven Lattice *73*
Woven Logs *72*
Woven Petals *218*
Wrapped Star (PatchDraw) *26*
Wreath *153*
Wreath (Rita Denenberg) *154, 162*
Wreath Stencil *139, 188*
Wren *131, 181*
Wren House *116*
Wright *75*
Wyoming Valley *41*

X

X *8, 9, 180*
x *180*
X (Foundation-Pieced Alphabet) *95*
x (Foundation-Pieced Alphabet) *94*
X is for Xylophone *215*
Xi (Greek Alphabet) *91*
xi (Greek Alphabet) *91*

Y

Y *8, 9, 180*
y *180*
Y (Foundation-Pieced Alphabet) *95*
y (Foundation-Pieced Alphabet) *94*
y acute (Foundation-Pieced Alphabet) *97*
Y Block *34*
Y Block Border *239*
Y is for Yo Yo *215*
y umlaut (Foundation-Pieced Alphabet) *97*
Yankee Puzzle *33*
Yellow Tulip *105*
Yod © Debbie Sichel *92*
You're #1 (Rita Denenberg) *170, 195*

Z

Z *8, 9, 180*
z *180*
Z (Foundation-Pieced Alphabet) *95*
z (Foundation-Pieced Alphabet) *94*
Z is for Zebra *215*
Zayin © Debbie Sichel *92*
Zero *8, 10*
Zeta (Greek Alphabet) *90*
zeta (Greek Alphabet) *90*
Zig Zags Border *237*
Zig Zags Corner *237*
Zig Zag Border 2 *238*
Zig Zag Border 3 *239*
Zig Zag Border 4 *239*
Zig Zag Border 5 *239*
Zig Zag Corner 2 *239*
Zig Zag Corner 3 *239*
Zig Zag Corner 4 *239*
Zig Zag Corner 5 *239*
Zinnia *185*
Zinnia Ring *197*
Zoe Fish *159, 184*
Zorro Fish *160, 184*